Hibiscus

Hibiscus

Hardy and Tropical Plants for the Garden

Barbara Perry Lawton

Timber Press
Portland • Cambridge

Published in 2004 by
Timber Press, Inc.
The Haseltine Building
133 S.W. Second Avenue, Suite 450
Portland, Oregon 97204-3527, U.S.A.

Timber Press
2 Station Road
Swavesey
Cambridge CB4 5QJ, U.K.

www.timberpress.com

Printed in China

Library of Congress Cataloging-in-Publication Data

Lawton, Barbara Perry.
    Hibiscus : hardy and tropical plants for the garden / Barbara Perry
Lawton.
        p.   cm.
    Includes bibliographical references (p.   ).
    ISBN 0-88192-654-X (hardcover)
1. Hibiscus. I. Title.
    SB413.H6L38   2004
    635.9'33685–dc22

                                    2003027747

A catalog record for this book is also available from the British Library.

To my children,
with great appreciation for their encouragement.

Contents

Color plates follow page 80

Foreword

It is not easy to write about a single group of plants. It takes a special talent to remain focused on the details of individual species and cultivars and at the same time to make the writing interesting and informative. This is especially challenging with such a diverse collection of plants as those of the genus *Hibiscus*. As a group, members of *Hibiscus* have been studied as annuals, perennials, or shrubs and trees, but fans of the genus have been hard-pressed to find a single reference in which the facts and folklore can be found at a single sitting. Finally, Barbara Lawton has done just that, providing details about the tough rose of Sharon, the many hardy *Hibiscus* species planted as perennials in gardens, and the tropical forms that can be used as garden annuals or to beautify homes. Each chapter is filled with information about history, breeding, useful cultivars for the gardener, and design applications. Barbara has provided an understanding of breeding, taxonomy, and the details of propagation. However, while she is obviously a keen fan of *Hibiscus*, she does not hesitate to point out the sad but necessary truths about garden problems, such as the pests and diseases associated with this group of plants. This book will educate and fascinate and is destined to become a standard reference for the genus.

Allan M. Armitage
Athens, Georgia

Preface

My earliest memories of hibiscuses come from the so-called road movies starring Bing Crosby and Bob Hope. In films such as *The Road to Bali,* Dorothy Lamour became known as their sarong-clad sidekick. A sultry brunette, she is often quoted as having described herself as "the happiest and highest paid straight woman in the business." Lamour's ever-present signature, in addition to the sarong, was a luscious white tropical hibiscus worn behind one ear.

With her body-sculpted sarong and trademark hibiscus, Lamour became a well-known image of the 1940s. We kids learned that wearing a hibiscus over the left ear meant that you were available and that wearing one over the right ear meant that you weren't. Or was it the other way around? No matter—I never wore a hibiscus, and neither did anyone else I knew. Perhaps we led sheltered lives. Nevertheless, the more I have learned about hibiscuses, the more I have enjoyed them.

I originally wanted to write a book about the entire family Malvaceae, of which there are some 116 genera and 1550 species of cultivated plants. Now that I've looked more closely at the genus *Hibiscus,* I am content to keep my horizons a little less expansive. It is a great enough challenge to cover this genus adequately.

Delving into *Hibiscus* is like unfolding an intricate puzzle. At each turn, more leads appear, more hints of paths not yet taken,

and more names of people who have over the years been inti-
mately connected to the genus in one way or another. There are
the collectors who found *Hibiscus* species throughout the tropical, subtropical, and warm temperate regions of the world. Then
there are the taxonomic botanists who continue to untangle the
web of plant relationships in this genus. Plant breeders, yet
another group of people with close ties to these plants, have
found hibiscuses to be genetically malleable and easy to breed.
As a result, attractive new varieties are brought into cultivation
every year, and gardeners have an increasing number of sensa-
tional tropical and hardy hibiscuses from which to choose.

In searching for the histories of various hibiscuses, I came
upon a number of dead ends, leaving me with apparently unan-
swerable questions as to who was involved in breeding certain
varieties. Since horticulturists do not keep the same kinds of
records as do taxonomic botanists, I went in circles around the
country, via e-mail and telephone, trying to trace the background
of cultivated hibiscuses, especially the hardy perennial types.
Only with a lot of help was I finally able to learn about the background of many cultivars.

One of the things I love about the hardy hibiscus is its tough-
ness. Once established in a compatible environment, it will thrive
in spite of whatever Mother Nature throws at it—snow, ice,
drought, flood, poor soil. If ever there were an optimistic plant,
this is it. It flourishes for years, bearing its bright flowers as if to
flaunt any adverse conditions. Its only fault is that it is a total slug-
abed. When spring comes and the hardy hibiscus doesn't, inex-
perienced growers think the plant has died. It hasn't. It will begin
to grow again as soon as all threats of chilly air and soil are past.
Be patient—the wait is well worth it.

The sight of our native American hibiscuses, with their summer crowns of white, red, and pink blooms, must have astounded
early explorers. I myself am still astonished when I see the hibiscus colonies of nearby marshy areas all in bloom on a summer
day. One August day in Route 66 State Park outside of St. Louis,

I just about fell off my bicycle when I came around a bend and saw colonies of *Hibiscus lasiocarpos* growing in low spots all along the trail. The white flowers with their rosy eyes punctuated the 6-foot (1.8-m) stalks abundantly.

Not long after this, I drove past the original entrance of the Missouri Botanical Garden and saw the pure white flowers of the hardy *Hibiscus* 'Blue River II' in the raised beds that accent the old stone gate. The morning sun highlighted the snow-white flowers and it was a spectacular sight—golden light on glistening petals.

More recently, on a visit to a farm belonging to an Amish couple in central Illinois near Arcola, I was surprised to see more than 400 hardy hibiscuses in 5-gallon (19-l) containers next to the family's greenhouse. It was late September and these plants were blooming their heads off, 4-inch (10-cm) red and pink flowers nodding in the breeze. I presume these were *Hibiscus moscheutos*. The woman had grown them from seeds her daughter had sent from Indiana.

It's odd, isn't it, how once you are launched on a particular subject, you keep running across examples that you never expected to find.

Acknowledgments

Once again I owe thanks to Peter Raven, director of the Missouri Botanical Garden, who provided both valuable botanical contacts and encouraging words. Thanks must also go to the garden's many staff members, who have been generous with their knowledge and experience, and to the employees of the garden's library, always patient and immensely helpful. I particularly appreciated Heather Wells-Sweeney, who found many of the illustrations used in this book, helped photograph the color plates, and assisted with my research.

A number of knowledgeable people provided horticultural, botanical, and taxonomic information, including *Hibiscus* expert

Paul A. Fryxell of the University of Texas. Mary Walters of Walters Gardens and Karen Park Jennings of Park Seed Company were kind enough to point me in the right direction on hardy cultivars. Robert Dirig and Sherry Vance of the Bailey Hortorium, Cornell University, helped with some of the history. George and Kay Yatskievych, both of the Missouri Botanical Garden, provided information and photographs. Deb Lalamondier led me through the wilds of the Missouri Botanical Garden's Climatron to find some dandy tropical hibiscuses. Akio Seki of Sakata Seed Corporation in Japan helped me research the background of various cultivars. Cindy and Doug Gilberg of Gilberg Perennial Farms were constant sources of information and encouragement.

Carl Scharfenberg, Wendy Bergman, and Mark Smith of Yoder Brothers, a research and production farm in Alva, Florida, taught me much about the commercial breeding of *Hibiscus rosa-sinensis* and *H. moscheutos* varieties. Hibiscus breeder Gordon Fore, past president of the American Hibiscus Society and former nursery owner, provided helpful information on the history of tropical hibiscuses. Keith Emery, plant pathologist and grower of tropical hibiscuses in St. Louis, helped me learn more about contemporary tropical hibiscuses. Rob Griesbach, a research geneticist with the U.S. Department of Agriculture at Beltsville, Maryland, was of tremendous assistance, filling me in on the background and history of many hardy perennial hibiscuses.

I was both thrilled and thankful to receive a long letter from Harold F. Winters, the breeder of one of my favorite hardy selections, *Hibiscus* 'Blue River II'. Winters was able to fill in many blanks in the background of hardy hibiscuses and their cultivars. Thanks are also owed Alan Whittemore of the U.S. National Arboretum, who pointed me in the right direction on the hibiscuses bred by Robert Darby.

Additional photographs were generously provided by Doug Gilberg, Ken Gilberg, Jack Jennings, the Kuwait National Museum, and the St. Louis Art Museum.

This is my second book published by Timber Press, and I must say that the people at Timber are like favorite family members. From the editorial department through marketing and publicity, they are a joy to work with.

And finally, my thanks to Allan Armitage, one of my favorite garden writers, for providing such an inviting foreword.

The Genus *Hibiscus*

What is it that is so fascinating about the classic hibiscus flower? The pure clean colors and flared bells of our contemporary tropical and hardy varieties are grand assets, as is the beauty of many original species. The plants of this genus have much to offer. In addition to having spectacular flowers, they are vigorous, tough, easy to grow, and long-lived. Who could ask for more in an ornamental plant? And hibiscuses are enjoying an era of increasing popularity, as garden designers and home gardeners alike discover and rediscover their attributes.

By recent count about 220 species of annuals, perennials, herbs, shrubs, subshrubs, and trees belong to the genus *Hibiscus*. This book covers many of those that are well known horticulturally or commercially. This is a genus of great diversity. Some hibiscuses originated in tropical regions of the world, others in temperate regions. Some are herbaceous, others woody. In habit they range from low-growing, spreading types to upright, woody forms that reach up to 30 feet (6 m) tall.

The flowers of most species open early in the morning and begin to droop and wilt by late afternoon. Most last only one day, but a few varieties have flowers that last two days or more. While most hibiscus flowers are odorless, a few are modestly fragrant, including *Hibiscus arnottianus* and *H. waimeae*. Flowers range in size from a prim ½ inch (1.25 cm) up to flamboyant floral platters that measure 12 inches (30 cm) or more in diameter. A wonderful bonus to growing hibiscuses is that many of them attract hummingbirds and butterflies.

Hibiscus is the largest genus in the mallow family (Malvaceae), a group of some 116 genera, many of which are economically valuable. Plants of this family share certain flower characteristics. There are five petals, and these are equal in size and separate, though they may overlap. The filaments are fused, forming a tube that encircles the style. Five-ribbed seedpods are also characteristic. Overall, mallow flowers tend to be either funnel- or plate-shaped. Some hibiscuses bear flowers with recurved petals. The flat flowers have sometimes been compared to windmills—not a bad metaphor, when you think about it.

The genus *Hibiscus* has lost a few members due to improvements in botanical technology. In the past, taxonomy was based on the physical characteristics of the flower parts of a plant. Now the ability to analyze genetic structure is providing even better ways to understand the relationships that exist among plants. Some plants that were once included in the genus *Hibiscus* have now been moved elsewhere.

From a gardener's point of view, the two main types of hibiscus are hardy and tropical. The hardy hibiscuses available to gardeners derive from a few species, mostly North American natives such as *Hibiscus coccineus* and *H. moscheutos*, while most tropical hibiscuses descend from *H. rosa-sinensis*, which originated in Asia. Hardy hibiscuses and tropical hibiscuses are discussed in separate chapters.

Rose of Sharon (*Hibiscus syriacus*) is the hardiest hibiscus of all. In addition to being a true shrub, and a very hardy one at that, rose of Sharon fills quite a different role in the garden—as a background planting, screening, or hedge, for instance. In this book, this species and its many varieties are addressed separately from other hardy hibiscuses, most of which are herbaceous perennials.

The hardiness zone map located at the back of the book indicates average low temperatures during winter months for the various parts of the United States. Zone information is also provided in chapter 10, "A Gallery of Hibiscuses," which lists and describes individual species and cultivars. Information about hardiness zones is good to know, and often a good place to start when selecting plants, but it is not a dictate. As adventurous gardeners have discovered, many plants can be successfully grown beyond their zonal limitations. Some of this is due, of course, to the vagaries of winter. Missouri, where I live, is rated as Zones 5 and 6, but I have known winters that would qualify for Zone 4 and winters that would qualify for Zone 7. If you want to grow hibiscuses that are not rated for your zone, find a site in which they will not be exposed to winter winds or extreme low temperatures. Your property may include microclimates that can shelter plants from these conditions. Planting near a wall or foundation may also have a tempering effect.

A number of color plates and black-and-white illustrations in this book were found in the magnificent works assembled at the Missouri Botanical Garden Library. Together, they make a handsome historical record of plants that stretches back to the earliest days of printing. For a list of the books and publications in which the illustrations appear, see "Further Reading."

Chapter 1

Hibiscus in North America

More than a dozen hibiscuses are native to North America. This chapter describes the best-known species, including those native to moist sites in eastern North America and those native to more arid sites in western North America.

The eastern species are herbaceous perennials found growing in damp, marshy, or even wet situations from Florida north as far as New York and west to Nebraska and even Minnesota. All are hardy to Zone 5, and the toughest among them are hardy to Zones 3 or 4. These species have been bred and crossbred into handsome, sometimes startling new hybrids.

The western species grow in Mexico and the desert Southwest of the United States. As you might guess, these plants require a lot of sun and good drainage, especially during winter months. Most have smaller flowers than their moist-soil cousins. They are not as tough, either, requiring the kinds of temperatures found in Zones 7 to 11. Although these dry-land natives often do poorly in the more humid and rainier parts of North America, they are often as handsome as some of the better-known species of moist or even wet sites.

The western hibiscuses are not cultivated much and can be difficult to find. However, they often bloom in their first year if grown from seed and started early, so this may be the way to enjoy them if you don't live in desert lands. Search for seeds through seed exchanges and seed houses that specialize in plants of the desert Southwest. These hibiscuses have not often been used in the hybridizing and selection of garden species. I expect they may be garden stars in the future should someone come along with an interest in breeding them. That someone would be well forewarned to recommend the resulting cultivars for arid regions similar to these plants' native lands.

Natives of Eastern North America

Swamp hibiscus (*Hibiscus coccineus*) is a tall, woody perennial with three-, five-, or seven-lobed leaves that are smooth and glaucous. The deep red summer flowers grow singly in upper leaf axils and are up to 6 inches (15 cm) wide. This hibiscus grows in coastal swamps and tidal marshes from Florida to Georgia.

The great rose mallow (*Hibiscus grandiflorus*) is another tall woody perennial native to southeastern coastal swamps and marshes. As the species name suggests, its late summer flowers are large, up to 6 inches (15 cm) in diameter. These are pink, white, or rosy purple, sometimes with a crimson eye. The three- or five-lobed leaves are broader than they are long.

Rose mallow (*Hibiscus lasiocarpos*), with its softly hairy stems and leaves, is native to wet areas and shallow water from Florida to Illinois and Missouri. The showy summer flowers, 4 to 6 inches (10 to 15 cm) across, grow singly in leaf axils and are white or rose with a magenta to crimson eye. Leaves grow on long petioles and are somewhat cordate and pointed at the tips. Considering how much interest there has been in water gardens, I'm surprised that hibiscus breeders have not been using *H. lasiocarpos* in their programs. This hardy shrub would thrive in wetland gardens, at the edges of ponds, or even in shallow water.

Halberd-leaved rose mallow (*Hibiscus laevis*) is a native of riverbanks, marshes, and swamps from Pennsylvania to Minnesota and south to Florida and Texas. The lower leaves of this gla-

brous, woody perennial are cordate to ovate, while the upper
leaves are three-lobed, with the middle lobes very much the
longest, giving the leaves a lance-like appearance. Flowers are
off-white to pale pink with a dark red eye. This species is increasingly included in breeding programs.

Swamp rose mallow (*Hibiscus moscheutos*) has been used in
breeding programs more than any other species. It is a robust,
tall, woody perennial found in brackish or fresh marshes and
damp places. The mid-green leaves are whitish and downy on
their undersides, ovate to lanceolate, and either unlobed or shallowly lobed in three or five parts. The summer flowers, 6 to 8
inches (15 to 20 cm) in diameter, grow singly in leaf axils and
may be white, pink, or rose, with red bands at the base of the petals. Subspecies *moscheutos*, native throughout the southeastern
United States, has white or, less often, pink flowers with a red
band around the base. This subspecies has been used as a parent plant in breeding programs that have brought us the white-
flowered 'Blue River II', pink-and-white-flowered 'Cotton Candy',
scarlet-flowered 'Poinsettia', crimson-flowered 'Southern Belle',
and pink-flowered 'Radiation'. The Disco Belle hibiscuses are
dwarf forms of 'Southern Belle'. Subspecies *palustris* has pink or
rose, rarely white, flowers with no red band at the base.

Natives of Western North America

The heartleaf hibiscus (*Hibiscus cardiophyllus*) is noted for its ability to attract hummingbirds and butterflies. Its cordate leaves
are handsome, as are its red to orange-red flowers with yellow
stamens.

Coulter hibiscus (*Hibiscus coulteri*) is a shrubby plant with yellow to pale yellowish white flowers. Once established, it is a prolific bloomer.

Paleface rosemallow (*Hibiscus denudatus*) is another native of
the desert Southwest. Its white to pinkish to lavender flowers are

small for this genus and grow on short stems in upper leaf axils. The foliage is covered with yellowish fuzz, and the leaves are ovate and finely dentate.

Chapter 2

Notable *Hibiscus* Cousins

If you are studying hibiscuses, you may find it worthwhile to take a look at some of the other notable plants in the same family. The mallows (Malvaceae) are native to temperate and tropical regions around the world. Many are useful as ornamentals; others are valued sources of fiber, food, and even medicine. Once you become familiar with the symmetrical, five-parted saucer or bell shape and prominent reproductive column of hibiscus flowers, you will see other plants with a similar look to their blossoms. Look closely at the flowers of hollyhocks, for example, and you might well guess that they are members of the Malvaceae. This chapter covers a few of the better-known *Hibiscus* cousins found in garden and agricultural settings.

Okra

A staple of southern and Creole cooking, okra is also a member of the mallow family and thus closely related to the genus *Hibiscus*. This mucilaginous mallow actually used to be placed in the genus *Hibiscus* but was moved when botanists honed in on its physiological characteristics. Formerly named *Hibiscus abelmoschus*, it is now *Abelmoschus esculentus*. It is also known as gumbo, gombo, lady's fingers, ochro, bamia, and bamya. *Gumbo*, derived from the Swahili word for "okra," is also often applied to the soups, stews, and other dishes that contain okra. *Lady's fingers* describes the look of the seed pods, though I can't imagine any woman wanting her fingers to be compared to these curious long green pods.

Okra appears to have been brought to North America from West Africa by slaves in the eighteenth century. Botanists believe that it originated in the region now known as Ethiopia. From there it may have been taken into Egypt and North Africa by Muslims from the east, who conquered Egypt in the seventh century. Okra appears to have been cultivated in Egypt as early as the twelfth century BC. From there it apparently spread throughout Africa and on to India and other lands to the east as well as around the Mediterranean. The pods were cooked and eaten, and the seeds were toasted, ground, and used to make a drink not unlike coffee. Indeed, this concoction continues to be used as a coffee substitute in Africa and the Middle East.

Many southern vegetable gardens include okra, which grows 2 to 8 feet (0.6 to 2.4 m) tall. The plants are coarse perennials from the tropics and must be grown as annuals in most parts of the United States. The pods are ready for harvest only about sixty days after the seeds are sown. Continually harvesting the pods when they are 3 to 4 inches (7.5 to 10 cm) long will ensure a continuous crop. Okra pods are ready to be picked four to five days after the flowers fade and drop off. When at their best for eating, they are a rich green, tender but firm, and snap in half easily. They get tougher as they mature. The young leaves of okra plants may also be eaten.

Among the best okra varieties are 'Clemson Spineless', an All-America Selection winner; 'Dwarf Green Long Pod', a fast grower with ribbed pods; and 'Annie Oakley', a compact plant that is more tolerant of cool weather.

While okra is fairly resistant to pests and diseases, it may be susceptible to fungal problems. Flea beetles, Japanese beetles, cucumber beetles, and corn earworms may be found on okra but seldom reach worrisome levels. Aphids may be a problem as they collect on the undersides of the leaves, but these can be washed off with a fine hard spray of water. As with any plant, it pays to monitor carefully for signs of damage.

Okra can be dried for later use. In the Mediterranean, ripe seeds are sometimes harvested for the oil they contain, which is excellent for use in cooking. The leaves are used in some places, including Turkey, to prepare a poultice for soothing and reducing inflammations. Okra is even occasionally used to make paper and rope.

Flowering Maple

Flowering maples (*Abutilon* species) are also known as Chinese bellflower, Indian mallow, Chinese lantern, and parlor maple. These deciduous, tender shrubs and small trees originated in Brazil, tropical Asiatic regions, and the tropical regions of India. They are widely admired for their beautiful saucer- or bell-like flowers and handsome foliage.

Although there are an estimated 16 recognized species in this genus, the flowering maple most often encountered in nurseries and botanical garden displays is *Abutilon* ×*hybridum*, which has been bred and selected into many attractive varieties, with flowers ranging from white to yellow, orange, red, and even blue. The foliage, usually a solid pale green, may also be variegated with yellow or white mottling.

The handsome *Abutilon megapotamicum* makes a fine houseplant, with its red and yellow pendulous flowers and leaves that are cordate at the base. A variegated form is also available, as are a number of cultivars.

Although flowering maples may be grown outdoors in Zone 8 or warmer, they are most often grown as houseplants. When grown outdoors they thrive in full sun with an average garden soil. While they may reach 10 feet (3 m) tall and wide, they can easily be kept at a smaller size through judicious pruning and by pinching back the growing tips. Since these plants grow easily from cuttings, you may want to try growing 3- to 5-inch (7.5- to 12.5-cm) prunings taken in spring to summer.

When grown indoors, flowering maples should be provided shade, filtered shade, or morning light. Good drainage, moderate watering, and regular but light applications of fertilizer will assure good growth. In plants that are short of nutrients, the lower leaves die. Be careful in your diagnosis, however, as problems with lower leaves can also be due to overwatering. These plants can be grown outdoors during warm seasons but must come back inside before frost.

Flowering maples kept as houseplants will probably have to be restrained through pruning and pinching so that they do not take over the room. It helps to keep them root-bound in a slightly smaller pot than the root ball would normally require. Pruning is best done in late fall or early spring.

Hollyhock

A tip of the hat is owed hollyhocks (*Alcea* species), even though these plants are not of great economic importance. In ancient China, hollyhocks were grown both as ornamentals and food. The cooked leaves and buds are still considered a delicacy by many country people, and the flowers have been a garden favorite for hundreds of years. The earliest remains of hollyhocks were found in the grave of a Neanderthal man, carbon-dated to about 50,000 years old.

It is known that hollyhocks have been grown as garden ornamentals since at least the fifteenth century, because they were mentioned in a poem of that time. By the middle of the seventeenth century, a number of varieties had been selected and named, in a wide range of colors and in both single- and double-flowered forms. The English brought hollyhocks to America in the early seventeenth century. Thomas Jefferson grew them in his Monticello gardens. These plants adapted so well to their new land that volunteers soon appeared everywhere, giving rise to the nickname "alley orchids." *Alcea rosea* is the best known of the eight species, and the one most often found in gardens. It probably originated in Turkey or Asia.

Hollyhocks are loved and admired for their tall, majestic stalks that bear a profusion of saucer-like or double flowers from late June through September. The flowers range from the purest white to nearly black, in just about every color but blue, and are sometimes a combination of colors or have white margins or centers. The round flat seedpods are often called cheeses because they resemble wheels of cheese. The word *hollyhock* may derive from *holy*, in reference to the Crusaders who brought the plants to England, and from *hoc*, meaning "mallow."

Hollyhocks may be annuals, biennials, or short-lived perennials. Most are biennials that begin to grow from seed in summer, then bloom and die the following year. Grow hollyhocks in full sun to partial shade in well-draining soil of moderate fertility. They reach 6 to 8 feet (1.8 to 2.4 m) tall, making them excellent background plants and effective against a wall or fence. Shorter cultivars are also available.

Hollyhocks are a must for old-fashioned gardens and can be easily grown from seed. As soon as they are established, they are likely to self-sow, making it unnecessary to plant seeds every year. Make sure to thin out the seedlings so that they are 6 to 10 inches (15 to 25 cm) apart, depending on the mature size of the variety.

Cotton

Although there are an estimated thirty-nine species of *Gossypium*, native to tropical and temperate regions of the world, only four are economically significant: Pakistani-Indian cotton (*Gossypium arboreum*), South American cotton (*G. barbadense*), African-West-Asian cotton (*G. herbaceum*), and Mexican cotton (*G. hirsutum*). The most important is *G. hirsutum*, which predominates in commercial cotton production throughout the world. Cotton's great economic importance is due to its capacity for being woven into yarns for a variety of fabrics. It is strong, absorbent, and lends itself well to dyeing. Washability and durability make cotton fabrics common, popular, and comparatively inexpensive around the globe.

Pakistani-Indian cotton (*Gossypium arboreum*), also known as tree cotton, has been used by natives of the Indus Valley to produce textiles for at least 4000 years. This cotton has been selected into several cultivars, some of which are short annuals and some of which are tall perennial shrubs. Two millennia ago, one of the perennial cottons was introduced to the Meroe tribes of Nubia, whose people became skilled weavers (in fact, they are considered Africa's earliest weavers). This cotton spread throughout Africa and led to Nigeria becoming a cotton-manufacturing center in the ninth century.

South American cotton (*Gossypium barbadense*), also called Sea Island cotton, originally grew in tropical South America along both the Atlantic and Pacific coasts. Today, in the wild, it is found in a more restricted area: the coastal region of Ecuador. This cotton has been introduced into cultivation in many parts of the world. Archeological digs in the desert country of northern Chile have uncovered the oldest recorded South American textiles, dating back to approximately 3600 BC. Archeologists working sites along the coast of Peru have found signs of the domestication of South American cotton in ancient cotton bolls that are clearly intermediate forms between the original native cotton and modern forms of this species. Cotton agriculture spread throughout South America and into the West Indies. By the 1650s cotton had become a major slave plantation crop in Barbados. This was the first British West Indian colony to export cotton. Around 1670, *G. barbadense* was introduced to Britain's

North American colonies, and it is now grown off the southeastern coast of the United States.

African-West-Asian cotton (*Gossypium herbaceum*), also known as levant cotton, is thought to originate in South Africa but was probably domesticated in Ethiopia or southern Arabia. Its cultivation spread throughout east-central Africa, Asia, and India. Growers selected superior plants that could be grown as annuals. The first known cultivation in China occurred around AD 600.

Mexican or upland cotton (*Gossypium hirsutum*) originated as wild populations growing along the coasts of southern North America, Central America, the West Indies, and even on some Pacific islands. Archeologists have found bits of cotton boll and fiber from the Tehuacán Valley of Mexico that are thought to be about 7000 years old. The Mayan and Aztec civilizations were among those who cultivated cotton throughout the Central American and Mexican lowlands. Early Spaniards observed cotton being grown in the 1500s. The Aztecs valued strips of cotton textile called *mantas*, and Montezuma demanded cotton *mantas* as tributes from his provinces. Cotton appears to have been cultivated in the southern part of North America by AD 100, as evidenced by cotton seeds found in Arizona during archeological digs. As cotton agriculture spread north from Mexico, growers increasingly selected annual forms of the plant, forms that could grow and mature in the long hot summer days of what is now the southern United States.

The history of cotton plantations in America and their partnership with slavery is well known. When slavery was abolished in the British Empire in 1835, British mills began looking to the United States for raw cotton. Cotton production grew until American plantations supplied 80 percent of the British mills' annual production. Cotton growing was revolutionized as a result of the Civil War, the abolition of slavery, and the Industrial Revolution. Cotton today, like wheat and corn, is a monoculture crop that is highly mechanized, often irrigated, and that uses great quantities of fertilizers and pesticides.

While *Gossypium hirsutum* continues to be the most important cotton species, some specialty cottons that have been developed have outstanding virtues and command greater value. *Gossypium barbadense*, for example, has lustrous white fibers that are longer than those of any other cotton and that can be spun into very fine yarns. American-Egyptian cotton, or Pima, is a hybrid with especially long fibers. It is grown commercially in irrigated lands of the southwestern United States.

Cotton's flower buds are called "squares" because of their general shape, even though they're typically five-parted. Once the bud opens and the flower is fertilized, the ovary develops into an oval boll. Once the boll matures, it splits and the long white seed hairs appear. Each of these fibers, collectively called "lint," is connected to one of the numerous brown to black seeds. When mature, each fiber is flat, thin, and tubular, with a spiral twist. Fibers range in length from ½ to 2½ inches (1.25 to 6.25 cm).

In addition to being one of the world's most valuable sources of fiber for textiles, *Gossypium hirsutum* plays other roles in its long relationship with humankind. Cottonseed oil, extracted from the seeds, is used in margarine, cooking and salad oils, and as a protective coating for machinery and tools. Cottonseed meal or cake, which consists of what's left after the oil is extracted, is a rich source of protein used to feed livestock; it is also used in human foods, though to a lesser degree. Low-grade cottonseed meal serves as fertilizer and fuel. The fibers left over from ginning are used in many commercial products, from felt, carpet, surgical cotton, twine, and mattresses to rayon, plastic, shatterproof glass, and cellulose explosives.

In folk medicine, cottonseed and the roots of cotton have been used to treat bronchitis, diarrhea, and hemorrhage. A decoction of the roots has been used to treat asthma and dysentery. In modern medicine, parts of *Gossypium hirsutum* are used to treat nasal polyps, uterine fibroid growths, and certain types of cancers. In China an extract of the plant serves as a male contraceptive.

Weedy Relatives

Every family has a black sheep or two, and the mallows are no exception. The best-known pernicious mallow weed is called cheeses (*Malva neglecta,* formerly *M. rotundifolia*) because of its round, cheese-like fruit. It is also known as round-leaved mallow and low mallow. Native to northwestern Africa and southwestern Asia, this plant has successfully naturalized in North America.

Cheeses are annual or biennial plants with straight taproots and procumbent stems. The mostly hairy leaves are circular and simple or shallowly lobed. Pink or white, single or clustered, ½-inch (1.25-cm) flowers appear in the leaf axils. These plants grow easily from seed. They can be in flower and producing seeds from June through October.

These weedy invaders are all too common in new lawns, farmyards, cultivated ground, roadsides, and waste places. The best defense is to remove them by hand or hoe them when they are small. Large plants that are in flower and in fruit should be pulled and destroyed.

Chapter 3

History, Traditions, and Uses

When a plant has played a role in the lives of people for a very long time, century upon century, an explanation of exactly how and when it all began is often necessarily nothing more than an educated guess. It's true that stories, traditions, and lore are often anecdotal and so can't be proven one way or another. It's also true, however, that we have to take a great deal of our knowledge on faith or theory. This is the case with the history of certain members of the mallow family, especially the China rose (*Hibiscus rosa-sinensis*).

The collections of the Missouri Botanical Garden Library proved to be a great resource in my search for the history of hibiscuses. William Curtis's eighteenth-century publication, *Curtis's Botanical Magazine*, yielded marvelous color illustrations, including a drawing of the annual or short-lived perennial *Hibiscus trionum* (Plate 1), an Old World native of arid tropical regions, and a drawing of a blood-red form of the ever-popular *H. rosa-sinensis* (Plate 2).

At the herbarium of the Missouri Botanical Garden, I was able to find two herbarium sheets from the late eighteenth or early nineteenth century. Both sheets came to Missouri in 1857 as part of the collection of a recently deceased German professor, Johann Jakob Bernhardi. The botanical garden purchased the entire 60,000-plant herbarium for the bargain price of $600.

The first sheet holds a specimen of *Hibiscus coccineus* that was cultivated in Philadelphia (Plate 3); the second holds rose of Sharon (*H. syriacus*), also cultivated in Philadelphia (Plate 4). Both were collected by unknown persons. The plant specimens are in amazingly good shape considering their age, but the labels are incomplete and inadequate by modern standards.

History and Customs

The word *hibiscus* derives from the ancient Greek *hibiskos*, the name for the plant known as marsh mallow or white mallow. As far as is known, the Greek physician Dioscorides bestowed the name on the marsh mallow in the first century AD. Marsh mallow (*Althaea officinalis*) is a perennial that grows up to 6 feet (1.8 m) tall. Though it originated in Europe, it is also widely naturalized in the eastern United States. Its flowers are white to pale lilac or pink, and its leaves are broadly ovate to triangular-ovate and either entire or shallowly crenate. Its mucilaginous roots are traditionally used in confectioneries and as a demulcent.

Long ago in Egypt, hibiscus flowers were thought to promote lust. The ancient Egyptians believed that tea made with red hibiscus flowers and calyces would induce licentious cravings in women. As a result, for many centuries women were forbidden to drink hibiscus tea.

Since ancient times, the signs of the zodiac have been linked with animals, colors, precious stones, metals, and plants. Aquarius, for instance, is associated with all the bright colors of the rainbow because these are the colors of Uranus, the ruler of the sign. Aquarius is also represented by hibiscuses, orchids, and pelargoniums.

Hibiscuses play an unusual part in the cultural traditions of Caribbean countries. Here the flowers are often carried in wedding bouquets, as they are believed to ward off bad luck.

Plants of the genus *Hibiscus* have been known of in the gardening circles of the Western world since the late 1600s. One

European illustration of the China rose (*H. rosa-sinensis*) dates back to 1678. There is evidence that this Asian native was introduced to the Chelsea Physic Garden in London in 1731. Interestingly, although early references agree that the China rose did originate in China, it has never been found there in its wild form. Quite probably because the plant reached its greatest development as an ornamental plant in China, it was given the name *rosa-sinensis*. In addition, the single form of the China rose was very rare in China in early times. The single red form was reported growing wild on the Malabar Coast of India, but there has been disagreement as to whether that was actually this species. Since the early history of this plant was never recorded, the true story is lost in the haze of history. Carolus Linnaeus classified the species in *Species Plantarum*, published in 1753.

Art

Hibiscuses appear on porcelain plates made in China that date back at least as far as the Ming dynasty (1368–1644). A Jingdezhen ware dish with a hibiscus spray design, dated to the Hongzhi period of the Ming dynasty, can be viewed in the Chinese art collection of the Art Gallery of New South Wales. Hibiscuses also appear in many silk tapestries made in China.

Hibiscuses, quite probably varieties of *Hibiscus rosa-sinensis*, are prominently featured in the art of the Mughal Empire (1526–1858), which included much of India, Bangladesh, and Pakistan. Elements of nature—flowers, fruit, foliage, trees, birds, animals—are profusely illustrated in Mughal books, paintings, textiles, and architecture. The lidded cup and saucer pictured in Plate 5 are a good example of art from this period. Only 3.25 inches (8 cm) tall and 5.25 inches (13 cm) in diameter, the gold and enamel cup is either Mughal or Deccan in origin and dates to about the mid-seventeenth century. The swirling pattern is characteristically Mughal, and the motif is of a tropical hibiscus.

The hibiscus bud is depicted in the process of unfurling with one petal extended. The handle of the cup lid is a hibiscus bud, ruby red with a golden calyx. This beautiful cup and saucer are fabricated from gold decorated with floral motifs on a background of white enamel. According to the curator at the Kuwait National Museum, where these elegant pieces are kept, they are among the finest examples of this kind of intricate work. This highly developed Indian style of overpainted enamels probably developed in and spread from the prolific art center of Hyderabad in the Deccan Plateau region of India.

The best-known Mughal architectural monument is the Taj Mahal in Agra, built in memory of Mumtaz Mahal, adored wife of Shah Jehan. Many floral motifs can be found in the bejeweled marble carvings of this majestic building. Hibiscus is among the flowers depicted and elaborately inlaid with agate, lapis lazuli, carnelian, and other multicolored stones and gems on the main grave in the central chamber.

Antique prints have become very popular among collectors and decorators, and listings can be found on various Web sites. At the time of this writing, a hand-colored copper engraving of *Hibiscus cameronii* that first appeared in Joseph Paxton's *Magazine of Botany*, published in London from 1839 to 1841, is listed at $115. A hand-colored etching of *H. mutabilis* that appeared in Henry C. Andrews's *The Botanist's Repository*, published from 1797 to 1815, is listed at $145.

Postimpressionist Paul Gauguin often celebrated tropical hibiscuses in his paintings of Tahitian women. He painted the first of his many portraits of native women shortly after his arrival in Tahiti in 1891. In *Vahine no te Tiare* (Woman with a Flower), a white flower in the subject's dark hair is just visible against a yellow background. It wasn't long before the painter fell in love with a Tahitian woman named Tehamana. He would paint her again and again, often with a hibiscus as her only adornment.

Hibiscuses have been featured on postage stamps as well. Santa Lucia issued a 1996 stamp portraying *Hibiscus elatus*, and stamps featuring other hibiscuses have been issued by Cuba (1969), North Vietnam (1964), and North Korea (1960, 1967, 1975).

The hibiscus has also appeared in haiku, a form of poetry that originated in Japan in the seventeenth century. Matsuo Bashō (1644–1694) is credited with having developed haiku as an important art form. Among his many haiku is this:

> As for the hibiscus
> on the roadside—
> my horse ate it.

Classical haiku contains a seasonal reference and embodies both simplicity and directness. It consists of three lines of five, seven, and five syllables, respectively, as Bashō's haiku undoubtedly does in the original Japanese.

Geography

Hibiscuses are noted and honored in name in several places. The Hibiscus Coast, which stretches along KwaZulu-Natal from Hibberdene to Port Edward, has some of the finest resorts and beaches of South Africa. Though originally named for the hibiscuses native to the area, the association has become a bit hazy in modern times. The area is now known as a top tourist destination, offering deep-sea fishing, scuba diving, golfing, and gambling.

Another Hibiscus Coast can be found in New Zealand in Auckland's Rodney District. Named for native hibiscus trees (possibly *Hibiscus heterophyllus*), the region is also widely known as the playground of Auckland. Like the Hibiscus Coast of Africa, this Hibiscus Coast has become known for its tourist attractions, including golf courses, restaurants, shops, a world-class marina, thermal pools, and surfing and swimming beaches.

The island of Jamaica celebrates the hibiscus in its name, which in Spanish means "hibiscus." *Jamaica* actually originated as an Indian word meaning "island of springs" but later came to be synonymous with the flower. In Hispanic shops in the St. Louis region, I ask for jamaica when I want to buy hibiscus tea. This tea mainly comes from Mexico.

China rose (*Hibiscus rosa-sinensis*) is the national flower of Malaysia, where it is known as bunga raya. It was introduced to Malaysia, probably from China, many centuries ago, possibly even before the twelfth century. In addition to its role as an ornamental, this hibiscus has been used extensively in medicine. Malaysia's first prime minister, Tunku Abdul Rahman, chose the China rose as his country's national flower in 1960. The red of the flowers stands for courage, while the five petals represent the country's Five Principles of Nationhood.

Hibiscus brackenridgei has become the most widely planted shrub of the tropics and subtropics. In June of 1988, nearly thirty years after becoming the fiftieth state of the United States, Hawaii officially adopted the pale yellow form of this species, known to Hawaiians as pua aloalo, as its state flower. This may be the same hibiscus that is the national flower of Key West, known fondly as the Conch Republic.

Rose of Sharon (*Hibiscus syriacus*) has for many years been the national flower of South Korea, where it is known as mugung-hwa. *Mugang*, meaning "endless," symbolizes Korea's perseverance, diligence, and its wish for national prosperity. The Koreans recognize the hardiness of rose of Sharon and its ability to produce 3000 or more blossoms on a single plant. Although Europeans first knew of this plant in Syria, it actually originated in eastern Asia, quite likely in China and India, where it was grown for centuries. It can be positively identified in early Chinese paintings and literature.

Hibiscus mutabilis originated in southern China but came to be known as the Confederate rose, thereby gaining a geographical association far removed from its native land. It was introduced into English gardens in the late 1600s and then into America in the nineteenth century, where it was widely used in southern gardens. Details of its travels to America are strictly narrative, but it is known that *H. mutabilis* was widely planted in Confederate cemeteries following the Civil War. It is said that southerners were so poor after the Civil War that they could only afford to decorate the graves of their relatives with the Confederate roses that grew so prolifically in their gardens.

Commercial Uses

Hibiscus cannabinus, or kenaf, is not a new crop plant. It was first planted and grown in sub-Saharan Africa more than 6000 years ago and has long been commercially grown in India, Africa, Asia, the Middle East, and more recently in Latin America. It has considerable potential as a crop in countries that fall within its tropical to subtropical requirements and could be grown in the southern United States as an environmentally sound alternative to soft and hard woods for paper production.

In the 1940s, when World War II choked jute imports from Asia, the U.S. Department of Agriculture began researching sources of fiber and chose kenaf from among 500 possibilities. After much research and many trials, kenaf paper has finally become available from several commercial manufacturers and retailers.

The U.S. Department of Agriculture considers kenaf an excellent alternative to wood-based papers for several reasons. In only 150 days, kenaf plants get to be up to 15 feet (4.5 m) tall. By way of contrast, the southern pines of many tree plantations require up to seventeen years before they can be harvested. Furthermore, kenaf yields up to five times more fiber per acre than southern pine, as much as 10 tons of dry fiber per acre. And once harvested, kenaf requires considerably less time, heat, and chemicals for processing.

Unfortunately, kenaf paper is currently more expensive to produce than wood-based papers. This is due to several factors, not the least of which are government subsidies to the timber, paper, and pulp industries. Start-up costs for kenaf-paper manufacturers also add to the cost.

Manufacturing kenaf paper would, in the long run, be cheaper not only in direct costs but also in costs to the environment. Forests would be spared, energy consumption lowered, and industrial pollution alleviated. Clearly, the development of kenaf agriculture and the manufacture of kenaf paper offer excellent alternatives to wood-based papers for the consideration of forward-thinking agricultural, governmental, and manufacturing leaders.

Kenaf is cultivated secondarily for the oil of its seeds, which is used in cooking, illumination, and lubrication as well as in the manufacture of soaps, paints, and linoleum. Once the oil is removed from the seeds, a concentrated seedcake can be made and used as cattle feed as well.

Like kenaf, *Hibiscus sabdariffa*, known as roselle, has the potential to be grown agriculturally in tropical to subtropical parts of the world, including in the southern United States. Its economic value is based on its dried calyces, which are used in many ways to create a number of edible products. They are brewed into teas and used to flavor juices, jams, jellies, and ice creams. Although the flower can be used as well, it is perishable, whereas the dried calyces are easily transported and have a long shelf life.

As herbal teas have grown in popularity, a greater volume of these dried calyces has been imported into the United States, with a reported increase in value of 156 percent from 1994 to 1998 (and from what I gather, the value has increased further since then). China is the major supplier to the United States, with Thailand, Mexico, and Egypt supplying smaller amounts. Oddly, the quality of the product varies considerably from year to year and depending on where it is grown. The stems of *Hibiscus sabdariffa* are also a rich source of fiber known as roselle hemp.

Traditional uses of hibiscus go back many centuries. Juice from the petals of *Hibiscus rosa-sinensis* was the source of hair dye, mascara, and shoe polish in early China and India. It has also been used to color liquors and to dye paper a purplish tint that reacts to alkaline and acid substances like litmus paper.

Edibility

Many plants of the Malvaceae, including hibiscuses, have been eaten as potherbs since early times, and modern researchers have discovered that some species are very rich in vitamins. Of course, extreme care should always be taken when introducing anything new to your diet. Even the comparatively innocuous genus *Hibiscus* has species that may irritate some people. The diuretic action of some hibiscuses, for example, might cause kidney problems in certain individuals. That said, if all necessary precautions are taken, you should be able to enjoy edible hibiscuses without problems.

The tender young shoots and fleshy leaves of cranberry hibiscus (*Hibiscus acetosella*) are tasty in salads and stir-fries. Cooked as a vegetable, they are good in combination with rice. The red coloring of the foliage and stems holds up well in cooking as long as they are not cooked very long—a light steaming works best.

The people of Chad eat the leaves of *Hibiscus cannabinus*, and the Chinese are known to have eaten the leaves of *H. mutabilis*, serving them boiled and seasoned with oil and salt.

Hibiscus sabdariffa can be used as a potherb. The leaves have a rhubarb-like tang and may be eaten cooked or raw, making good additions to stir-fries or salads. The seeds may be roasted and eaten or made into a sauce. The calyx can be made into a sauce very much like cranberry sauce (one common name for this species is Florida cranberry). The calyces are also used in preserves, chutneys, jams, and curries and make an excellent tea. In China the seeds are used for their oil.

The Chinese also serve the leaves of *Hibiscus syriacus* as a boiled vegetable seasoned with oil and salt. In the past the leaves were used as tea, and the edible flowers were considered a delicacy. In India the mucilage and stem bark of *H. tiliaceus* (syn. *Paritium tiliaceum*) are eaten and the stalks sucked.

In Hawaii, home to many tropical hibiscuses, the leaves are used in various ways. For example, to cook hibiscus greens, add the leaves to a pot of boiling water, remove the pot from the heat, cover it, and allow it to stand for five minutes. Avoid cooking the leaves too long or an okra-like mucilage will appear. Drain the water and, if desired, add butter and seasoning. The tender young leaves of edible hibiscuses can also be added to salads and stir-fries or used chopped or whole in meatloaf, pancakes, pot stickers, soups, stews, and tempura.

Medicinal Value

Use caution and consult a physician before using any hibiscus medicinally or for other health purposes. Pregnant women should avoid *Hibiscus* species altogether, as some appear to have abortive effects.

In general, *Hibiscus* species have been valued for their mild laxative properties and for their ability to encourage urination. Various Eastern and Western herbal medicines have been prescribed for constipation and mild nausea as well as for mild bladder infections. Hibiscus potions or extracts have been prescribed for external use to soothe sunburn.

Plants of the Malvaceae have been used medicinally from ancient times. Dioscorides, the first-century Greek physician and author of *De Materia Medica*, recommended that mallow leaves mashed together with a little honey and salt would cure fistulas of the eyes. He also noted that the same salve would soothe the pain from wasp and bee stings. A number of American Indian tribes used the root juices of mallow species to treat sore eyes.

John Gerard's 1633 *Herball* lists a number of medicinal properties ("vertues") for hibiscuses and their relatives. Although
many of the scientific names have changed since Gerard's time,
it is probably safe to assume that what he calls the marsh mallow
is either a hibiscus or a very close relative. According to Gerard,
the leaves of the marsh mallow have the power to ease pain. In
poultices they are used to treat any manner of pain, and the roots
and seeds have the same properties. The mucilage or slimy juices
of the roots mix well with oils, ointments, and plasters to treat
painful conditions. The roots, when boiled in wine and eaten,
expel stones and ease the pain of sciatica, cramps, and convul-
sions. Additionally, Gerard reported that the dried, powdered
seeds can be made into a drink that will stop the flow of blood.

The Chinese found that the China rose (*Hibiscus rosa-sinensis*) had astringent properties, meaning they could use its flowers and the juice from its petals to soothe irritated tissues, relax
muscle spasms, and check bleeding. Potions made from this Chinese hibiscus have been used by women for centuries to ease
painful and excessive menstruation and to treat venereal diseases
and cystitis. The Chinese also have a tradition of using this plant
to treat coughs and fevers. Oddly, decoctions made from the
China rose have also been used to encourage the growth of hair.

Ancient Indian texts recommend the flowers of *Hibiscus rosa-
sinensis* for its antifertility properties, and modern research seems
to support the recommendation. Scientific studies indicate that
the flowers have a significant antifertility activity, with the results
dependent on the stage of the pregnancy, the dose, and the
duration of the treatment. Extracts of the flowers also appear to
affect male fertility, but the use of this herb as a male contraceptive is unlikely, as it also seems to affect the libido.

Hibiscus aculeatus is an upright hairy perennial found in
savannas, pine forests, and along roadsides in the southeastern
United States from North Carolina to Texas. It was used by early
pioneers to make a tonic. The stems and roots were also prepared as a tea that was used to treat loneliness, melancholy, and

distress. For this reason the plant became known as comfort root.

Kenaf (*Hibiscus cannabinus*) has long been used as a folk medicine in Africa. It is said to be an aphrodisiac and a purgative. Africans use kenaf to treat bruises, bilious conditions, fever, and puerperium. Africans have also used peelings from the stems to treat anemia and fatigue. Ancient Indians used kenaf leaves to treat dysentery and blood and throat disorders. The seeds were used externally to treat aches and bruises and were also considered fattening.

The leaves of *Hibiscus moscheutos* can be used to make a gargle or soothing poultice. Tea made from the whole plant is a folk medicine that has been used to treat digestive and respiratory ailments.

Hibiscus sabdariffa is used as an internal tonic to treat kidney and digestive diseases and conditions. Like *H. rosa-sinensis*, it has astringent, cooling properties. It will help lower fevers and is useful as a diuretic. The healing properties of *H. sabdariffa* were traditionally believed to be many. It was credited with being antiseptic, aphrodisiac, astringent, digestive, diuretic, purgative, and sedative. It is used in folk medicine to treat abscesses, cancer, cough, dyspepsia, fever, hangovers, heart conditions, hypertension, neurosis, and scurvy. The people of Angola, Myanmar, and Guinea use the leaves as an emollient. The Taiwanese use the seeds as a laxative, diuretic, and general tonic. The people of the Philippines use the bitter root as a tonic. Central Africans use the leaves to make poultices for abscesses.

Chapter 4

Rose of Sharon

For many years I disparaged *Hibiscus syriacus*. I found it unattractive and scraggly, with sparse foliage and coarse branching, and despised the horrible, sickly, bluish pink flowers. I finally got my comeuppance when a nurseryman friend overheard my complaints and asked why I did not like rose of Sharon. I listed my reasons, to which he replied, "Why don't you try 'Diana'? Then let me know what you think."

Well, as you can guess, I became an enthusiastic convert to the contemporary rose of Sharon shrubs, with their robust, full foliage and branching patterns. 'Diana', for example, produces masses of white flowers all summer long until frost. It is a triploid cultivar, which accounts for its unusual vigor and extremely fine flowering pattern. Its growth pattern is handsome, and it is a tough shrub. All in all, I absolutely adore it. So much for early impressions.

Rose of Sharon has a number of assets that recommend it to gardeners. The single or double flowers that appear from late June to frost, 2 to 5 inches (5 to 12.5 cm) in diameter, are reliable and profuse, especially in the newer varieties. They range from white to red-purple to blue-lavender, usually with a crimson base, and unlike most hibiscuses, these flowers survive when cut for arrangements. The glabrous leaves average about 2 inches (5 cm) long and are shallowly three-lobed and coarsely serrate.

This shrub to small tree grows up to 12 feet (3.6 m) tall, and once established it will thrive with little attention, even in hot, dry weather.

History

Known primarily as rose of Sharon, *Hibiscus syriacus* is also called althea, shrub althea, Syrian ketmie, Syrian rose, and tree hollyhock. For more than four centuries this hardy shrub has been a popular member of English gardens, bearing its flowers from June to autumn, when few other shrubs exhibit color.

Linnaeus named this species in the eighteenth century, supposing that it had originated in Syria. In truth, rose of Sharon is native to eastern Asia, probably originating in India and China.

English herbalist John Gerard grew the plant from seed in 1597 and called it the tree mallow. In 1759 there were seven kinds of rose of Sharon, including two variegated specimens, in the Chelsea Physic Garden in London. Thomas Jefferson planted seeds at Shadwell in 1767, then in spring 1794 installed specimens of the plant in beds at Monticello. In the nineteenth century most nurseries in the southern United States carried rose of Sharon, and it became the most popular nursery plant in the South. By this time there were nearly two dozen named varieties of both single- and double-flowered varieties. The American 'Admiral Dewey', noted for its pure white double flowers, remained popular for many years.

William Robinson described the virtues of rose of Sharon on a number of occasions in his weekly journal, *The Garden*. In a September 1847 issue he noted that the shrub, in bloom, "forms a fine contrast to the somber foliage by which it is everywhere surrounded." Some years later, in 1897, he described the plant as "a beautiful shrub, bearing large showy blossoms in late summer and in autumn, when shrubberies would otherwise be flowerless."

Hibiscus syriacus (Salisbury et al. 1805–1807). Courtesy of the
Missouri Botanical Garden Library.

Victor Lemoine, a well-known French nurseryman, introduced several rose of Sharon cultivars into the marketplace. His 1873 catalog included three cultivars, and by 1909 he had increased that number to nine. He bred some of these himself, while others came from a source in the United States.

Hibiscus syriacus 'Meehanii', a variegated shrub, has long been grown in Europe.

Modern Breeding

The late Donald Egolf was working at the U.S. National Arboretum in Washington, D.C., when he made a number of breakthroughs in breeding rose of Sharon. From 1959 until his death in 1990, he was in charge of the shrub-breeding program at the arboretum. By this time plant breeders were using colchicine, a poisonous alkaloid derived from autumn crocus (*Colchicum autumnale*) and used to alter the number of chromosomes in hybrids. The increased numbers of chromosomes resulted in larger, more substantial, longer-lasting flowers.

Egolf used this technique in his hibiscus breeding programs and developed tetraploids. These plants had larger flowers, but there were fewer than Egolf wanted. Consequently, he crossed the tetraploids with diploids and ended up with triploids. These were extremely floriferous and produced large flowers. In addition, these rose of Sharons proved to be sterile.

Egolf released *Hibiscus syriacus* 'Diana' (1970), 'Helene' (1980), 'Minerva' (1986), and 'Aphrodite' (1988), all named after Greek goddesses and all triploids. These were the results of crosses between diploid seedling selections of 'Suminokura-yae' × 'William R. Smith', 'Blue Bird' × 'Hanagasa', or 'Sokobeni-yae' × 'William R. Smith' and colchicine-induced tetraploid seedlings of 'William R. Smith'. 'Diana' is 8 feet (2.4 m) tall and 7 to 8 feet (2.1 to 2.4 m) wide with dense branching, has pure white 4- to 5-inch (10- to 12.5-cm) flowers in profusion, and blooms continuously from June until frost. It was developed from a cross between a tetraploid seedling with white petals and a red eye, and a heavily ruffled white diploid seedling. The cross was made in 1963, and the triploid plant first flowered in 1964. The flowers of 'Aphrodite' are mauve with a magenta eye. 'Helene' has white flowers with a dark red center. 'Minerva' is a well-branched smaller form with violet flowers that grows to about 8 feet (2.4 m) tall and 7 feet (2.1 m) wide. Egolf also bred the rose of Sharon called 'Blue Bird', with pale, nearly true blue flowers.

A variegated *Hibiscus syriacus* with semi-double, peony-like flowers was introduced by Hillis Nursery in McMinnville, Tennessee, in 1993. Called 'Hillis Variegated', it was first discovered as a sport on the parent plant. It is similar to the parent species except that it is slightly less hardy. This is typical of variegated forms, since they have less chlorophyll. The flowers are more than 2 inches (5 cm) in diameter and first appear as showy candy-striped buds, opening to pale pink flowers.

Sometimes sheer luck and chance come into play in the discovery of new forms of old favorites. Such was the case some years back when plantsman Don Shadow imported a shipment of *Hibiscus syriacus* from Japan. In that shipment was an unnamed rose of Sharon with dusky dark pink flowers. The flowers were double but edged by single-form petals. Shadow named his discovery 'Freedom'. 'Boule de Feu' is another double-flowered cultivar worth considering. Though not a new cultivar, it is gaining interest just the same.

Lavender Chiffon ('Notwoodone') and White Chiffon ('Notwoodtwo') are impressive cultivars that were introduced in the late 1990s. Both were bred by physiologist Roderick Woods of Cambridge, England, who was looking for a good pink-flowered rose of Sharon when he happened upon these unusual varieties. Woods retired from a career in physiology and histology to breed *Hibiscus syriacus* cultivars—yet another example of a dedicated amateur gaining good results in the business of plant breeding. Gardeners in temperate climates are fortunate to have Woods working on their behalf: he has come up with a whole new look for rose of Sharon flowers. Lavender Chiffon and White Chiffon have 4- to 5-inch (10- to 12.5-cm) double flowers with lacy centers that make them look somewhat like anemones. Interestingly, in the double flowers the style and stamens are formed like petals. Both plants reach 6 to 8 feet (1.8 to 2.4 m) tall and wide at maturity.

Around the end of the twentieth century, four stunning new cultivars of *Hibiscus syriacus* were introduced, trademarked as Satin hibiscuses. Two of these, Blue Satin ('Marina') and Blush Satin ('Mathilda'), were bred by Dutch plantsman Rien Verweij in an attempt to improve on 'Blue Bird' and 'Hamabo'. The other two, Rose Satin ('Minrosa') and Violet Satin ('Floru'), were bred by Claude Bellion of Minier Nurseries, France.

As recently as the 1970s, rose of Sharon plants were sold primarily by their color rather than by any other special characteristics. Few plant breeders had any idea of the scope and variety of color and form that would become available in the coming years. It was Donald Egolf's colchicine-induced varieties that pointed the way to today's elegant rose of Sharon cultivars. When 'Aphrodite', 'Diana', 'Helene', and 'Minerva' came onto the scene, gardeners and garden designers alike suddenly realized that this was no longer a scraggly shrub with insipid pinkish lavender flowers. The new varieties are sturdy, well-shaped woody plants with magnificent blooms, worthy of a respected place in any garden. And the Egolf varieties proved to be just the beginning of the new age for rose of Sharon. A list of the most popular cultivars of this species can be found in chapter 10.

England established a National Collection in Woodbridge, Suffolk, in 1984 under the direction of Ivan Dickings, the propagation manager at Notcutts Nurseries. In 1995 the National Collection included some thirty-three named cultivars of *Hibiscus syriacus*, plus a few known only by numbers and by the names of their breeders.

Cultivation

Hibiscus syriacus is the hardiest ornamental hibiscus. Fully hardy to Zone 5, this tough woody plant will grow in full sun to partial shade and will tolerate extremes of heat and cold, surviving subzero temperatures with ease. It is also tolerant of a wide range of soil conditions, although it will perform at its best only when given a moist, fairly organic soil that drains well, with a pH of 5.5 to 7.0. In soils of greater acidity, rose of Sharon may become chlorotic, a condition easily cured by adding agricultural lime to the soil. This plant tolerates salt air and is thus a good choice for seaside locations. It is also easy to transplant. It does best in colder climates, where it is at its most vigorous. In warmer climates, including southern Florida and southern California, tropical hibiscuses may be a better choice. Rose of Sharon cultivars will thrive in ordinary soil and full sun to partial shade and are hardy in Zones 5 to 8.

Most nurseries carry containerized shrubs, which means that these shrubs can be planted whenever the soil can be worked. Plant the shrub at a level that is slightly higher than where the plant was situated in the container. Regular applications of an organic mulch should provide ample nutrients. Rose of Sharons can also be fertilized in late winter or early spring with a commercial fertilizer formulated for flowering plants.

Rose of Sharon grows at a slow to moderate pace, eventually reaching 8 to 12 feet (2.4 to 3.6 m) tall and 4 to 6 feet (1.2 to 1.8 m) wide. It seldom needs pruning if planted in a large enough spot—simply pruning away any broken or dead branches should be enough. Any pruning that is needed is best done after the shrub finishes blooming, in late fall or very early spring, before the plant leafs out. This shrub blooms on new growth, so pruning should be scheduled so as to guarantee ample time for flower bud development. If a rose of Sharon must be cut back hard, prune away about half of the bush. It won't look very attractive for some time, but it will recover. Some gardeners prefer to treat rose of Sharon in the same way as forsythias, cutting back about a quarter of the growth all the way to the ground each year. This results in what amounts to a new plant every four years. With the modern cultivars, I prefer to avoid pruning unless absolutely necessary and have yet to find them becoming unsightly.

There are few problems with pests and diseases. Aphids and red spider mites occasionally appear on young tender growth, but these are easily controlled with a fine hard spray of cold water from a garden hose. Applications of insecticidal soap are another good control.

Design

Most popular flowering shrubs bloom in spring. Use the bold shrubby forms of rose of Sharon in shrub beds and borders to provide added color from summer through fall.

As a specimen plant, rose of Sharon is most appealing when planted where it is not in full view—its winter look is a bit gaunt, and the new growth does not appear as early as that of most shrubs. On the other hand, rose of Sharon is superior for screening swimming pools or disguising unsightly fencing. It is also a good choice to plant against a large bare wall.

Through calculated pruning, rose of Sharon bushes can be trained into standard forms with single or triple trunks. Simply choose the strongest of the stems, then regularly strip off any growth below the level of 3 to 4 feet (0.9 to 1.2 m).

Because of its rather coarse open growth, the species is most valuable as a background shrub or as a hedge faced with shorter fuller plants. It also makes a good choice for screening narrow side yards.

A number of new cultivars have thicker, less open growth habits than the species and are therefore much more attractive and useful in the landscape. Among the best of these are 'Diana', 'Helene', 'Minerva', and 'Aphrodite'. The foliage of these triploids is more robust and of a richer green than the species. Watch for new cultivars—a number of promising new varieties have popped up recently. Dwarf varieties are also becoming available, each growing to a maximum height of 3 feet (0.9 m).

Chapter 5

Hardy Hibiscuses

In recent years hardy hibiscuses have become the bright shining stars of summer gardens, their sunny faces a cheery sight in containers, beds, and borders. They are available in an expanding variety of colors, foliage and growth patterns, and flower sizes—with some flowers reaching mind-boggling proportions. Horticulturists have made great strides in breeding these tough plants into new forms. All are hardy to at least Zone 5.

The leaves of hardy perennial hibiscuses are matte and usually medium green. Flowers are white, pink, red, or some subtle combination of the three and up to 12 inches (30 cm) in diameter, much larger than those of a tropical hibiscus. The large size of the flowers is due in part to genetics, but temperature also plays a role. Flowers are largest when summer temperatures are at their hottest. Likewise, cooler weather results in smaller flowers.

History

The garden history of hardy hibiscuses derived from North American natives is short when compared to the history of the China rose (*Hibiscus rosa-sinensis*) and its closely related tropical hibiscuses. *Hibiscus moscheutos* and *H. coccineus* were probably brought into American gardens and exported to England and other European countries as early as the 1700s. America's first great botanist and plant collector, John Bartram (1699–1777), certainly would have included native hibiscuses in the plant collections that he distributed to his contemporaries in both the United States and England. These American hibiscuses captured people's attention with their extremely large flowers.

In 1807 the Philadelphia company John Bartram and Son listed both *Hibiscus moscheutos* and *H. palustris* (now *H. moscheutos* subsp. *palustris*) in its catalogs (Winters 1970). In 1820, William Prince of Flushing, Long Island, was also selling these native hibiscuses. He added *H. militaris* (now *H. laevis*) to his sales list in 1822, *H. grandiflorus* in 1825, and the *H. moscheutos* varieties *alba*, *pallida*, and *rubra*, which are no longer recognized, in 1827.

Kept in the Bailey Hortorium Library at Cornell University, a 1902 catalog from Peter Henderson of New York describes some perennial hibiscus cultivars of that time. Henderson referred to these plants as marsh mallows, describing them as "hardy garden plants forming strong bushes about 3 feet [0.9 m] high, bearing throughout the summer immense saucer-shaped flowers 6 inches [15 cm] across. Sown early they will flower the first season." Among the cultivars for sale were 'Giant Yellow', with garnet-eyed, canary-yellow flowers often 9 inches (22.5 cm) across; 'Crimson Eye', with flowers marked by a crimson center; and 'Rose Pink with White Base', with exquisite rose-pink flowers with a white center. The parentage of these cultivars is unclear.

One early hibiscus hybridizer was Ernest Hemming of the Thomas Meehan Nursery, Philadelphia. Although he couldn't have known much about genetic compatibility as we do today, he successfully crossed *Hibiscus coccineus* with *H. militaris* (now *H. laevis*) and in 1903 obtained a red-flowered seedling that successfully grew in his region. Meehan then crossed this hybrid with *H. moscheutos*, and within a few generations he had some remarkable results. His plant selections had flowers that varied from white to white with a red eye, to light and deep pink, scarlet, and dark red.

Furthermore, the leaf shapes varied from entire to deeply cut. His seedlings were first sold in 1907 as Meehan Mallow Marvels by the Thomas Meehan Nursery. These hybrids are still available through some nurseries, listed as *H.* 'Mallow Marvels'.

Modern Breeding

Beginning in 1952, Louisiana native Sam E. McFadden, a staff member at the Florida Agricultural Experiment Station, University of Florida, Gainesville, developed a program for breeding hardy hibiscuses from existing named cultivars, including those listed as Mallow Marvels. In 1962 the agricultural experiment station introduced a successful new cultivar, *Hibiscus* 'Flare', which was bred when McFadden crossed the perennial *H.* 'Brilliant Cerise', obtained from a California source, with *H. moscheutos* seedlings.

Two well-known hardy cultivars, *Hibiscus* 'Southern Belle' and 'Dixie Belle', were bred by the Sakata Seed Corporation's Chigasaki breeding station in Japan. Both were bred from common rose mallow (*H. moscheutos*) and Confederate rose (*H. mutabilis*). 'Southern Belle' was bred in the late 1960s, and 'Southern Belle Mix' was introduced to the marketplace in 1971. 'Dixie Belle Mix' was bred in the late 1970s and introduced in 1980. 'Dixie Belle' was discontinued in 1991 and is no longer available.

Sakata Seed Corporation also bred the Disco Belle series at its Chigasaki breeding station, beginning in the late 1970s and continuing into the late 1980s. The parents of these hibiscuses are the same as for 'Southern Belle'. The main difference is that the Disco Belle hibiscuses are smaller. 'Disco Belle White' was introduced in 1982, 'Disco Belle Rosy Red' in 1985, 'Disco Belle Mix' in 1989, and 'Disco Belle Pink' in 1993.

Robert Darby bred *Hibiscus* 'Lord Baltimore', 'Lady Baltimore', and 'Anne Arundel' from the 1950s through the 1970s, all diploids named in honor of early Maryland settlers. Reproduced by cuttings and divisions, these cultivars continue to be popular.

'Lord Baltimore' was the earliest variety, a chance seedling that first bloomed in 1955 and was not patented. One of the parents was of an old series known as Avalon Hybrids. A near-sterile hybrid that bloomed continuously from July until frost, its ancestry probably included *Hibiscus laevis*, *H. coccineus*, *H. moscheutos*, and *H. moscheutos* subsp. *palustris*. It is considered by many to be the best red-flowered hibiscus.

'Lady Baltimore' produced its first flower in 1972 and received its patent in June of 1978. Its seed parent is 'Lord Baltimore'. Its pollen parent is unknown but was selected from open-pollinated progeny of 'Lord Baltimore' or selected pink-flowered hibiscuses. It is an elegant plant with good landscaping qualities. It has large pink flowers and deeply lobed foliage.

'Lady Baltimore' became the seed parent for 'Anne Arundel'. Pollen was taken from selected pink-flowered hibiscuses of several varieties, and the resulting seedlings were selected and back-crossed to eliminate poor qualities. 'Anne Arundel' produced its first flower in 1977, a clear pink bloom of great elegance. The patent was awarded in March of 1984. The plant is medium in size with good form and habit—another good landscaping choice.

In the late 1950s and early 1960s, Robert Pryor, who worked at the U.S. Department of Agriculture Plant Introduction Station in Glendale, Maryland (now located in Beltsville), made some interesting crosses of hardy hibiscuses in his garden. He was most interested in developing dwarf varieties, but because these types were not popular during that time, his hibiscuses never gained much attention. Too bad! There has been a lot of excitement about dwarf cultivars since the beginning of the twenty-first century—Pryor's hibiscuses would have been received with open arms.

Harold Winters also worked at the Plant Introduction Station in Glendale, where he was involved with plant collections from all over the world, organizing and participating in expeditions and seeing to it that plants got to the appropriate breeders, growers, and researchers. Winters was unable to patent his cultivars because he worked for the U.S. Department of Agriculture, but from the late 1960s through the 1980s he bred hardy hibiscuses in his home garden, including the wonderful *Hibiscus* 'Blue River II' and 'Sweet Caroline'. The white-flowered 'Blue River II' is a cross of *H. laevis* and *H. moscheutos*. It was named after the Blue River in southeastern Oklahoma, not far from Durant, where Winters found *H. laevis* growing. The pink-flowered 'Sweet Caroline', introduced in 1993, originated as a seedling from a controlled cross. It is named after Caroline County, Maryland, where Winters owned a small farm. The ancestry of this cultivar includes *H.* 'Super Clown', *H.* 'Plume', and *H. moscheutos* subsp. *palustris.*

Winters learned the technique of using colchicine to alter plant chromosomes from Donald Egolf of the U.S. National Arboretum, but it is unclear as to whether or not he used this technique in breeding hardy hibiscuses. His hibiscuses were introduced through the auspices of commercial nurseries like Wayside. It is doubtful if he ever recovered the costs of his breeding program.

The Fleming brothers of Lincoln, Nebraska, bred many fine hardy hibiscuses in their lifetimes. Jim, Bob, and Dave, each no more than 5 foot 5 inches (165 cm) tall, jointly established Fleming Flower Fields, where they hybridized hardy hibiscuses and other plants for more than half a century. Dave, the youngest brother and the last survivor, died in 2001.

Hardy hibiscuses were favorites of both Jim and Dave. The cultivars they created have large flowers, overlapping petals, excellent texture, and often unique foliage, including some with spoon-shaped leaves, others with hydrangea-like leaves, and still others with very finely dissected maple-like leaves.

The Fleming hibiscuses were bred, selected, and introduced from the 1970s through the 1990s. Most of these varieties derive from *Hibiscus moscheutos*, with a few descended from *H. coccineus*. Among the best-known cultivars are 'Kopper King', with red-streaked white flowers and copper-red foliage, and 'Old Yella', with pale yellow, slightly ruffled flowers with a crimson eye. 'Fireball' features purplish red foliage and large burgundy-red flowers.

The story of Morrison's Mammoth Hibiscus goes back to the 1970s, when William L. Morrison of Park Ridge, Illinois, a retired electrical engineer, began breeding hardy hibiscuses. It began one bitterly cold winter when Morrison's wife was designing her dream garden and wanted to include hibiscuses. That spring she charged him with buying a hibiscus plant—he chose a variety of *Hibiscus moscheutos*. Each year after that, the seed that fell to the ground grew into more hibiscuses of different sizes, colors, and blooming times. At first Morrison simply selected what looked like the best of the seedlings, but then he began to choose parent plants and cross-pollinate them to produce new varieties. He grew them in ordinary soil and with benign neglect. The results are tough, drought-resistant hibiscuses 3 to 6 feet (0.9 to 1.8 m) tall with magnificent flowers up to 12 inches (30 cm) in diameter. In the mid-1990s, Morrison contracted with Doug Gilberg of Gilberg Perennial Farms in Robertsville, Missouri, to be the licensed propagator of the Morrison's Mammoth Hibiscus series. The first cultivars of the series were 'Pyrenees Pink', 'Rainier Red', and 'Everest White'. 'Mauna Kea', 'Mt. Blanc', and 'Kilimanjaro Red' have also become garden favorites in much of the United States. 'Matterhorn' is an attractive variety with white and pink flowers. 'Etna Pink' has ruffled flowers and leaves with a reddish glow.

In the late 1990s, while Morrison was breeding his Mammoth Hibiscus series, Gilberg began searching for smaller, more compact hardy hibiscuses, especially those with unusual flower forms and new colors such as mauve or lavender. He was breeding mostly *Hibiscus moscheutos*, *H. coccineus*, and cultivars of the two. The first selection was 'Pitter Patti', discovered as a chimera—a single branch of pale pink flowers with scarlet veins was found on a red-flowered plant. Some of Gilberg's favorite new varieties are '100 Degrees', with light pink flowers; 'Mauvelous', with warm velvety mauve flowers; and 'Baboo', with white and pink flowers. All three are compact plants, reaching 3 to 4 feet (0.9 to 1.2 m) tall.

With the reborn popularity of hardy hibiscuses, I expect we will see many more wonderful new cultivars in years to come. They are being used more and more in private and public gardens and in park and municipal beds and borders, where they earn a well-deserved reputation for being easy to grow and maintain. These tough plants are now carried not only by specialty perennial nurseries but also by large chain stores, which sell them by the thousands each spring.

A detailed list of the most common hardy hibiscus cultivars can be found in chapter 10.

Cultivation

Hardy hibiscuses will not thrive in tropical or subtropical climates such as those found in southern Florida. They require a cold season to flourish, much as apple trees do. Nevertheless, once established, these hibiscuses can endure weather and environmental extremes amazingly well. They thrive in full sun with moist, fertile soil that is of good texture, producing maximum numbers of flowers when provided with six or more hours of sun each day. They are adaptable, however, and can tolerate ordinary soil, dry conditions, and some shade once they have recovered from transplanting. Since many of these floriferous beauties descend from plants that grow in wetlands, they are tolerant of wet soils, although, like many bottomland natives, they are also tolerant of droughty conditions. Hardy hibiscuses are not particularly fussy with regard to pH, adjusting well to the usual garden soil, which will probably be anywhere from 6.5 to 7.5.

Photoperiodism defines a plant's physiological response to day or night length. Changes of season often determine such events as seed germination and flowering. Plants determine the time of year by means of the relative lengths of night and day. This can be especially important for plants that are native to areas that are far from the equal nights and days of equatorial regions. Some plants, such as poinsettias and chrysanthemums, are initiated into flowering by short days and long nights. Others, such as beans, corn, and cotton, are day-neutral plants, meaning they are unaffected by the photoperiod. Still others are triggered into flowering by long days and short nights.

Hardy hibiscuses are considered to be long-day plants, but in actuality they are short-night plants. It has long been believed that their flowering is initiated by day lengths exceeding twelve hours. However, recent studies suggest that it is the comparatively short period of darkness that spurs the development of flowers.

Knowing about the native environment of a plant and then trying to match those conditions at home is the key to success with any plant. Learn what kind of climate and soil it thrives in where it is indigenous. If you are growing plants bred from or descended from species that originated in marshy locations in the eastern United States, you can confidently assume that your plants will be a good choice for soggy, poorly draining locations. If, on the other hand, the plants derive from species native to the desert Southwest and Mexico, the last place you will want to plant them is in a site with poor drainage. Given a few simple environmental conditions, depending on the species or on the origin of the cultivar, hardy hibiscuses are easy to grow, and reward gardeners with both the large size of their blossoms and the profusion of bloom.

Most hardy hibiscuses found in the marketplace are hybrids developed from species native to damp or even wet places in eastern North America, often in the same locations where cattails are found. These handsome ornamentals are hardy to Zone 5 or even Zone 4 but need to be treated as annuals in colder climes.

Of course, one never knows what winter will bring in the interior of the United States. The continental climate, not to mention the mountain chains that run north-south, means that northern winters may be as mild as those in Memphis or as severe as those in the Yukon Territory. Most winters are a combination of the two extremes. When people ask what the climate is like in St. Louis, where I live, I can truthfully tell them that it's too hot, too cold, too wet, and too dry.

Hardy hibiscuses are late to emerge in spring. In fact, I have known gardeners who pulled up their plants thinking that they had died over the winter. Be patient with these plants. They will begin to show some budding foliage well after most other plants are in full leaf.

These perennials can become gangly, so it is wise to give them a thorough tip pruning once the new spring growth is 18 inches (45 cm) tall. If they are growing rapidly, you may want to give them a second tip pruning to further encourage branching and bushy growth. But do not tip prune after the first of June or you will delay flowering too much. If you do not tip prune hardy hibiscuses once or twice to encourage branching and bushiness, the larger, more vigorous varieties may fall over in the summer unless you stake them or cage them. In most cases, however, these strong-stemmed hibiscuses rarely need to be staked.

Varieties that ordinarily reach a height of 6 feet (1.8 m) often set buds and flower at half that height. These are plants that respond well to pruning. Once the first flush of blossoms is past, encourage more blooms by trimming off the old flowers, including any developing seedpods. You should see new flower buds developing below the old ones. Don't make the mistake of over-pruning hardy hibiscuses once the first flush of bloom is past—this will delay the second round of flowers.

In fall, after a hard freeze, the foliage will die back, but it isn't necessary to prune the current year's growth until new growth begins in spring. The old growth, decorated with the last seed heads of the season, may provide winter interest. Similarly, some hibiscuses have red stems that keep their color well into winter. Most hardy hibiscuses are quite shapely if they have been tip-pruned during the growing season. If this is the case with your plant, leave it alone until new growth starts from the base in spring. At that time, prune back the old stems to 5 to 6 inches (12.5 to 15 cm) above the ground. If the plant becomes gawky or lopsided in late spring, go ahead and prune it back to 2 to 3 feet (0.6 to 0.9 m), shaping the plant as you do so; avoid, however, doing this after May. Dead, injured, and broken stems can be pruned out at any time of year.

Once there has been a hard freeze, put down 3 to 4 inches (7.5 to 10 cm) of mulch. There is no need to worry about root rot with these plants, since they originate from damp or wet places. The mulch will moderate temperature extremes, conserve soil moisture, and discourage weed growth.

Pruning hibiscus stems too close to the ground may open the roots up to damage from freezing. It also may lead to you forgetting the exact location of the plant. Never prune hardy hibiscuses to the ground midway through the growing season. The plants will not recover in time to set more blooms during that season.

Leave hardy hibiscuses in place for a decade or more. Don't bother trying to divide the crowns—a challenging task at best. It is far better to buy new plants or grow them from seed or cuttings. Just remember that if you do grow hibiscuses from seed, you probably won't get plants that are like the parents.

Design

Hardy hibiscuses often make superb centers of attention, grabbing the eye and eliciting excited oohs and ahhs from admirers. But since they are such big plants, with such big flowers, they often make the best impression when used as background plants at the far end of a property or as vigorous back-row features in perennial beds and borders.

Plantsman Tony Avent summed it up well in a recent bit of correspondence: "Plants such as hibiscus with large, flashy flowers have in the past been associated with gardeners who lacked good design taste. . . . Well, finally the mid-1990s arrived and, just like the mid-1960s, tacky was back in style. Even gardeners who had laughed at hibiscuses in the 1980s were now incorporating them in their upscale gardens. Hibiscuses are just like clothes fashions—if you wait long enough, they'll be back in style."

Their large scale makes many hardy hibiscuses top choices for big landscapes. Plant them about 3 feet [0.9 m] apart in a staggered row for hedges or massed plantings. They can also be combined well with many perennials, including ornamental grasses, daylilies, *Caryopteris*, and *Perovskia*. They make a fine addition to mixed beds and borders, blending in nicely with annuals and herbs, and make colorful summer focal points by an entryway or to accent a patio or porch.

Chapter 6

Tropical Hibiscuses

Though longtime favorites of gardeners in warm climates, tropical hibiscuses are comparative newcomers as indoor plants in colder climes of America, where they flourish in sunny windows and atria. During summer in temperate-zone gardens, these plants are bright spots in garden beds and focal points in containers. Although they are less buxom than hardy hibiscuses, with smaller flowers, 3 to 4 inches (7.5 to 10 cm) in diameter, their flowers are available in a wider range of colors and color combinations, including many shades of pink, yellow, orange, and red. Most tropical hibiscuses are noted for their glossy dark green foliage as well.

Tropical hibiscuses are now available in plant nurseries, chain stores, and supermarkets. They are bred by hybridizers in the United States (Florida, Texas, and California) and a number of other countries, including Australia and Tahiti. They have become so inexpensive that you can often buy them for less than it costs to buy a floral arrangement. The papery blossoms are usually open for just one day, but they keep developing throughout most of the year with just a bit of rest between flushes of bloom. In shape, the flowers are like funnels—steep or flat—and may be single or double. Petals may be entire or deeply cut and even feathered. Plant breeders continue to develop tropical hibiscuses in a kaleidoscope of colors and forms and are especially keen to find varieties with flowers that stay open for more than one day. In the wild, most of these plants want to be trees and will grow 10 to 15 feet (3 to 4.5 m) tall. Size will vary according to climate, growing conditions, and specifics of garden sites.

There are three basic horticultural types of tropical hibiscus on the market: florist-grade, outdoor-patio, and standard. These are merely terms of convenience, not botanical distinctions, used to describe the way these plants are grown to fill certain roles in the home or landscape. Growers for florists produce the florist-grade and outdoor-patio hibiscuses from cuttings. The standard or tree forms are grown by air layering.

Florist-grade hibiscuses are the tender, flowering, potted plants you see in flower shops, chain stores, and even grocery stores. These are comparatively small plants, usually no more than 1 to 2 feet (0.3 to 0.6 m) tall. One reason for this dwarfism is that many of the plants are treated with growth hormones that shorten the growth between leaf nodes and reduce the nitrogen that the plants take up. This creates the characteristic bushiness found among potted hibiscuses. In recent years plant breeders have been working toward developing varieties that are naturally dwarf and bushy so that growth hormone treatments will become unnecessary. Florist-grade hibiscuses have more flowers, foliage that is a deeper green, and denser growth. Growers begin propagating the plants in greenhouses in February to meet a spring marketing season. The plants are sold in hanging baskets and 6- and 10-inch (15- and 25-cm) pots.

Outdoor-patio hibiscuses are cultivated in extensive outside growing areas in warm climates and are not subjected to growth hormones. They are grown as bushes and are taller, have paler green foliage, and are more open in growth.

Growers are increasingly producing large numbers of ornamental standard tropical hibiscuses. When these stock plants reach a height of 6 to 8 feet (1.8 to 2.4 m), growers trim the branches so that each is just one long stem or trunk about 3 feet (0.9 m) tall. Then they wrap the lower part of the trunk with moist sphagnum moss and foil. When roots have grown into the moss, the growers cut the air-layered upper sections from the stock plants and place them in containers. The plants are trimmed and shaped into small trees. The entire process takes about a year.

History

The history of the tropical hibiscus is heavily oriented toward Asia, though there are also species native to Africa and Australia. The plants grown in the northern homes and southern gardens of the United States are mostly cultivars of China rose (*Hibiscus rosa-sinensis*), a complex species that has been grown in a variety of forms for many centuries. The species itself has never been found in the wild, and it has been grown for so long that its specific origin is not known. It is known, however, that people in India and China have been growing this plant in its many forms, both as ornamentals and as plants useful in their day-to-day lives, for many hundreds, even thousands, of years. Early European explorers apparently found many types of ornamental *H. rosa-sinensis* growing near Chinese palaces and temples.

Among the many common names given to *Hibiscus rosa-sinensis* is shoe black, a name provided by Portuguese explorers in reference to one way in which the plant was historically used in India. The flowers, when crushed, turn black and yield a purplish dye. In India this dye was used to stain shoes.

Daniel Solander, botanist to Captain James Cook, who had studied natural history under Linnaeus at Sweden's Uppsala University, made note of a hibiscus with double red flowers found in Tahiti in 1769. He called it *Hibiscus rosa-sinensis*, since Linnaeus had classified it in *Species Plantarum* (1753). This double-flowered *H. rosa-sinensis* is said to have first been grown in Europe by Philip Miller in 1731. Miller described the plant in an early edition of his *Gardeners Dictionary*. Some fifty years after the double-flowered hibiscus was introduced into Europe, the single-flowered *H. rosa-sinensis* began to appear in English greenhouses. By then, English horticulturists had imported other hibiscuses from China and were growing plants with double flowers in shades of buff, yellow, crimson, and even white.

The late Ross H. Gast, a research associate at the Los Angeles State and County Arboretum in Arcadia, theorized that, since the *Hibiscus* species that are cross-compatible with *H. rosa-sinensis* are found particularly in the Indian Ocean region on the islands of Madagascar, Seychelles, and Mauritius, *H. rosa-sinensis* is probably also from that region. He believed that the plant was later distributed into various Pacific regions by means of the Polynesian migrations. The Polynesian people themselves are often thought to have originated in India. The commonly accepted theory is that their migrations took the hibiscus to China and eventually around the entire Pacific region.

The common red hibiscus so often found in gardens of the southern United States is probably either *Hibiscus rosa-sinensis* 'Brilliant' or one of its close relatives. According to Gordon Fore, a past president of the Florida Hibiscus Society, 'Brilliant' was introduced to the United States from England in the eighteenth century at about the time of the presidency of George Washington. It is probably the oldest surviving variety known in the United States. It appears to have come to England from China—and, as Fore says, "only God knows when."

A resurgence of serious interest in *Hibiscus rosa-sinensis* began around 1900 in many places, including the United States (especially Hawaii and Florida), Fiji, India, and Sri Lanka. The breeding work that was done at that time suggested that this hibiscus is not in itself a species but a group of complex hybrids and their descendents. This means, of course, that hybridizing these hibiscuses offers a far wider range of possibilities than would be offered by a simple species.

Hibiscus collecting and breeding became very popular in the late 1990s, particularly in Hawaii. Hybrids of the compatible native Hawaiian and Asian species have resulted in a gigantic genetic pool of hibiscuses that continue to be developed into thousands of new cultivars. The excitement of discovering a new form or color combination, or a plant with greater vigor and disease resistance, should keep hobbyists and professional horticulturists breeding hibiscuses for many years to come.

Ross Gast was a major figure in the development of ornamental hibiscuses. He bred, selected, and introduced more than 3000 ornamental varieties of *Hibiscus rosa-sinensis* and explored throughout the world, looking for new species to use in his breeding station at the Los Angeles State and County Arboretum. Together with his close friend and hibiscus partner, Joe Staniford, Gast aimed to develop cultivars that would be tougher and more successful in southern Californian gardens.

As he traveled, Gast collected cuttings and seeds of hibiscuses that he thought would be compatible with those already in his collection. During those expeditions in 1963, 1965, and 1967, he wrote long letters to Staniford, now collected in the entertaining *Hibiscus around the World* (1980). Gast's travels took him to Britain, South Africa, the Mascarene Islands, Madagascar, and Reunion Island. The hibiscus collection in California grew to an immense size. Among other things, he noted that the breeding work that he and Staniford were doing at Arcadia indicated that the geographical range of hibiscuses can be extended through the selection of climactically tailored cultivars. For instance, frost losses are minimized when the cultivars planted are those with strong root systems resistant to low soil temperature and excess soil moisture.

Gast had lived in Hawaii in the mid-1930s and while there developed the Hibiscus Evolutionary Gardens at Waimea Falls Park on Oahu. He first became seriously interested in hibiscuses in 1946, inspired by the plants he had known in Hawaii. He became one of the founders of the American Hibiscus Society, and in the early 1980s he was honored by Hawaii for his many contributions to the state. He died in 1982.

Modern Breeding

The plant breeding business requires a lot of patience. It takes about one year from pollination to seeing the flowers and making selections. It takes another year to grow the plants big enough to take cuttings, and then these must be grown into decent-sized, marketable plants. Depending on how much branching you can force, it will take about three years to get 400 to 500 new cultivars of tropical hibiscus from seed to market. Apparently there are many who do have that patience—more than 6000 cultivars are registered with the American Hibiscus Society alone, to say nothing of registries in other countries.

Hibiscus rosa-sinensis is not the only ornamental tropical hibiscus with breeding potential. *Hibiscus arnottianus, H. cameronii, H. kokio,* and *H. schizopetalus* are also good candidates. Plant breeders have crossed these species with *H. rosa-sinensis* hundreds of times, resulting in thousands of cultivars. Of course, not all of these have been worth propagating and promoting to growers and gardeners. In fact, a breeder is lucky if one or two of every 200 crosses results in a handsome and vigorous new variety.

Hibiscus arnottianus, known as Wilder's white, is a shrub or small tree native to Hawaii. Flowers are 4 inches (10 cm) in diameter and surround a 6-inch (15-cm) red central column that bears slender stamens on the upper half to third. The slight perfume of the flower is a plus. This plant is often used in crosses with *H. rosa-sinensis,* so its genes can be found in many horticultural varieties. It is also used extensively as rootstock in grafting hybrids, because it is long-lived and has roots that are resistant to pests and disease.

Hibiscus cameronii, or pink hibiscus, is originally native to Madagascar but has long been cultivated as a hedge plant in Hawaii. It grows up to 6 feet (1.8 m) tall and is useful as an accent plant, shrub, or hedge. The attractive shrub form has often been used in hybridizing programs with *H. rosa-sinensis.* The flowers are pink, with darker shades at the base of the petals. Because the species is susceptible to root rot, its cultivars are often grafted onto stronger rootstock.

Hibiscus kokio, known as red hibiscus, is another native of Hawaii. It is a small tree or scraggly shrub with orange-red to red (occasionally orange or yellow) flowers with reflexed filaments. This is an endangered plant of the Hawaiian flora.

The exotic and beautiful *Hibiscus schizopetalus,* or Japanese lantern, is native to Kenya, Tanzania, and Mozambique. It has deeply split, recurved petals and a staminal column that is extremely long (longer than the flower's diameter). The flowers may be pink or red. I first saw this hibiscus growing in the Climatron of the Missouri Botanical Garden in St. Louis. The morning sun shone through the pendent flower—a lovely image.

Other modern tropical varieties that I observed in the Climatron were 'All Aglow', with yellow and caramel-brown flowers, and 'Fiesta', with flaming red and orange flowers. All were thriving in the controlled tropics of Buckminster Fuller's tetrahedron dome.

Florida has a concentration of tropical hibiscus breeders and is also home to the American Hibiscus Society. Some members dabble in breeding tropical hibiscuses and others just plain love the plants. Some hobbyist breeders go on to establish hibiscus nurseries, as with former American Hibiscus Society president Curt Sinclair and his Exotic Hibiscus nursery. After becoming involved in the society in the early 1990s, Sinclair became hooked on hibiscuses. His company now wholesales and retails hibiscuses throughout the world, from the United States to Europe, Japan, Tahiti, New Zealand, and the Philippines.

Sinclair grows his hibiscuses on their own roots and does not graft them. His crosses are made from various cultivars of *Hibiscus rosa-sinensis.* With the complex genetic structure of the China rose, says Sinclair, "I have a limitless gene pool at my fingertips." He grows more than 10,000 new seedlings each year, "waiting for those few silver bullets." Judging from what he has to offer, Sinclair has been very successful in developing tropical hibiscuses with larger flowers, up to 9 inches (22.5 cm) or more in diameter, and unusual colors or color combinations.

Only about 2 to 4 percent of the new blooms resulting from the crosses are chosen for testing. First Sinclair takes cuttings to see if they will root enthusiastically. The plants that pass this test go through a two- to four-year product development stage. About 75 percent of those will not make the grade.

Among the tropical hibiscuses carried by Exotic Hibiscus are 'Amanda Dubin', which has yellow flowers with a red eye; 'Blueberry Hill', which has pink flowers tinted a light blue; 'Byron Metts', which has pearl-white flowers; 'Chocolate High', which has caramel-chocolate flowers with a red and white eye; 'Miss Vermont', which has large red flowers tipped with orange; 'Texas Rose', which has bright lemon yellow flowers; and 'Wedding Band', which has burnt orange to reddish flowers edged in yellow.

Another company with a much longer history is Yoder Brothers, which established its Live Oak Farm, 22 acres of greenhouses near Fort Myers, Florida, in 1975 and now has the largest 6-inch (15-cm) hibiscus pot program in America. Yoder was originally founded by two Mennonites, Menno and Ira Yoder, in Barberton, Ohio.

I visited Wendy Bergman, the tropical hibiscus breeder at Live Oak Farm. She says she isn't looking for larger flowers but for "more flower production, strong glossy foliage, a strong mound form, dwarfism, and longer-lasting flowers." Bergman's TradeWinds series of tropical hibiscuses now includes more than two dozen cultivars, all with patents pending. Among the newer varieties are 'Candy Wind', which has pink, ruffled flowers; the notably compact 'Carolina Breeze', which has glowing orange flowers; 'Flaming Wind', which has soft red flowers with a dark red throat; and 'Golden Wind', which has yellow flowers with a light orange throat. 'Sundance' is a dependable variety that bears golden yellow flowers with a pinkish red eye. The flowers of the tricolor 'Mandarin Wind' are flame-orange with a pink band on the throat and a red eye. 'Captiva Wind' represents a color breakthrough, its pale lavender petals trimmed with pink outer edges. 'Cool Wind' has disease-resistant foliage and white flowers with a pink throat. 'Brilliant Red' is the best-selling Yoder Brothers hibiscus.

Some varieties of hibiscuses make better female parents and others make better male parents. For instance, in some cases the pistil pads may not be overt but are instead way down in the column. For this reason Bergman breeds new crosses both ways, using each plant as a female parent and again as a male parent.

In the past, growers have used growth regulators to dwarf hibiscuses, making the internodes between leaves much shorter. Extensive studies and breeding programs are making it possible to build in the dwarfism genetically rather than having to design a chemical series of treatments for each hibiscus crop.

Many tropical hibiscus experts, hobbyists, and breeders have found that there are too many variations of the same color and flower form being developed by people describing themselves as avid breeders. The late Harry Goulding, a noted breeder, used to say that if he got one good variety out of 5000 seedlings he felt very lucky. Goulding kept a notebook, what he called his "stud book," in which he kept records of all his crosses. Among his curmudgeonly sayings was, "If a parent plant keeps throwing throwaways, then throw away the parent—regardless of how great a seed setter it might be."

The Royal Horticultural Society has accepted the recommendation of its International Registrar that the term "tropical hybrids" be used for all the thousands of modern tropical hibiscus hybrids. The official definition is that the tropical hybrids as a group will include "*Hibiscus rosa-sinensis* and its sexually compatible species and its cultivars." This should solve a tricky taxonomic problem, especially considering there are more than 10,000 tropical hibiscus cultivars.

As to trying to guess at the most popular tropical hibiscuses, that's a bit like trying to pick one flavor of ice cream as everyone's favorite: ask a dozen people for the best hibiscus and you will get a dozen different answers. For this reason I have tried to mention only a few of the most notable tropical hibiscuses that I have heard about or run across in gardens and nurseries. A more comprehensive list can be found in chapter 10.

Cultivation

Tropical hibiscuses are hardy only to Zone 9 or less. They are commonly seen in warm-climate landscapes but are increasingly found in more northern climates as well, where they often spend summers outdoors and winters in homes and greenhouses.

Modern hybrids may grow on their own roots or may be grafted onto stronger rootstock. While some do well on their own roots, others are at their best only when grafted. Many experts recommend the grafted plants, reporting that they are more free-flowering, more vigorous, more disease-resistant, and more tolerant of environmental conditions. They may also have better growth patterns. On the other hand, plant breeders are constantly looking for new hibiscuses with great flowers and good growth patterns that will thrive on their own roots with no need for growth hormones or other special treatment.

Most tropical hibiscuses tolerate some shade but are healthiest and most productive in full sun. In tropical climates, these plants can be grown more successfully in partial shade than full sun. In cooler climates, when the plants are outdoors, they should have warmth, shelter from cool winds, and exposure to sun for at least six hours a day. Some species—*Hibiscus schizopetalus*, for example—do better if grown in half shade, so be sure to check the specific requirements for particular plants.

The best soil will have good drainage and texture and be highly organic with a pH between 6.2 and 6.5. If the soil is not of good quality, blend in compost or well-rotted manure. Regular mulching will help add organic matter to the soil, conserve moisture, moderate soil temperatures, and keep weeds from growing. Regularly mulch to a depth of about 2 inches (5 cm) as the old mulch decomposes.

Growing tropical hibiscuses in regions where winters are cold requires some special care. Potted plants must be moved indoors or to a greenhouse when threatened with freezing temperatures. In cold climates, prune potted plants in late winter or early spring. With clever pruning you can keep them at a reasonable size of 2 feet (0.6 m) or so. Indoors, the plants will probably get no more than three to four hours of direct sunlight each day. Supplemental lighting can help keep these hibiscuses healthy during the long cold season. When they get too little light, the signs are unmistakable—leaves will turn yellow and drop off. Keep the soil moist but be careful not to overwater. You can keep the humidity higher indoors by placing the pots on trays of gravel that are kept full of water.

Late winter is a good time to repot tropical hibiscuses if they need it. Use light soilless mixes of materials like peat moss, perlite, and vermiculite. Fine bark can be used to mulch the soil surface. Good drainage is the key to growing these tropicals.

Design

Tropical hibiscuses can be used outdoors as perennial shrubs in Zones 11 and 12 and in protected niches in Zone 10. These plants feature spectacular flowers, and some add color and contrast with variegated foliage. It is important to note that certain tropical hibiscuses have flowers that fade in full sun. Locate these varieties where they will receive only morning sun.

China rose (*Hibiscus rosa-sinensis*) and its cultivars are undoubtedly among the most popular outdoor plants in Hawaii, Florida, Malaysia, and other places with similar climates. As colorful foundation or base plantings, as specimens, or in groups or massed plantings, these tropical hibiscuses are beautiful work horses.

Japanese lantern (*Hibiscus schizopetalus*) is a good subject for hedging. It also works well for pleaching, an old English custom that involves interlacing twigs or branches to develop a densely growing screen above bare trunks.

As container plants, the tropical hibiscuses provide instant decor to patio, lanai, or doorstep. Standard forms also provide instant color and structure to the garden or home. However, while these containerized hibiscuses can remain indoors for a time, they will usually not get enough light to thrive. The best way to solve this problem is to have several hibiscuses that are rotated between the house and the garden.

Containerized hibiscuses are ideal for apartment and condominium dwellers who are short on space for gardening. The plants fit well on balconies and small patios. Grow them outdoors to keep them healthy, then bring them indoors for a while to decorate the home.

Tropical hibiscuses are likely choices for public plantings, simply gorgeous when planted along boulevard islands, beside highways, and in public parks. While the temptation is to use only the boldest colors, landscape designers would be well advised to consider the more subtly colored flowering hibiscuses. Imagine massed plantings of lemon-yellow hibiscuses flanked by plantings of white and pale peach. Sounds simply scrumptious, doesn't it? And it certainly would look a lot cooler than plantings of hot oranges and reds—a plus for tropical settings.

Plate 1. *Hibiscus trionum* (flower-of-an-hour) as depicted in *Curtis's Botanical Magazine* (Curtis 1793). Courtesy of the Missouri Botanical Garden Library.

Plate 2. *Hibiscus rosa-sinensis* (China rose) as depicted in *Curtis's Botanical Magazine* (Curtis 1792). Courtesy of the Missouri Botanical Garden Library.

Plate 3. This herbarium sheet holds a specimen of *Hibiscus coccineus* (swamp hibiscus) collected in Philadelphia in the late eighteenth or early nineteenth century. Courtesy of the Missouri Botanical Garden Library.

Plate 4. An herbarium sheet from the same collection. This one holds *Hibiscus syriacus* (rose of Sharon). Courtesy of the Missouri Botanical Garden Library.

Plate 5. This mid-seventeenth-century Mughal lidded cup and saucer are decorated with hibiscuses in gold and enamel. Photo by permission of the al-Sabah Collection, Kuwait National Museum, Kuwait.

Plate 6. Hardy hibiscuses are noted for their extremely large flowers. Photo by Ken Gilberg.

Plate 7. This artistic photo, taken from the underside of a hibiscus flower, clearly shows the veins of the petals, which straighten as the furled buds open. Photo by Jack Jennings.

Plate 8. Standard hibiscuses are increasingly popular.

Plate 9. Red-flowered hibiscus shrubs are common in warm-climate areas such as Fort Myers, Florida.

Plate 10. This pink-flowered hibiscus shrub serves as the perfect cover-up for a big utility box.

Plate 11. A hibiscus with pink, double flowers is an integral part of the foundation planting at this Fort Myers home.

Plate 12. Tip pruning of hardy hibiscuses results in bushier plants with more blooms. Photo by Cindy Gilberg.

Plate 13. Two to three weeks after tip pruning, this plant is bursting with flower buds. Photo by Cindy Gilberg.

Plate 14. The red stems of *Hibiscus* 'Etna Pink' hold their color well into winter and are especially attractive when snow is on the ground.

Plate 15. A rail fence is the perfect foil for this bed of hardy hibiscuses at the Missouri Botanical Garden.

Plate 16. *Hibiscus* 'Rainier Red' makes a splendid accent to the French doors of this Missouri home.

Plate 17. This hibiscus leaf was damaged by sawfly larvae.

Plate 18. Workers at Yoder's Live Oak Farm take tropical hibiscus cuttings and stick them into containers of growing medium.

Plate 19. A pot of tropical hibiscus cuttings. Putting several in one pot results in a bushier plant.

Plate 20. A test field of hardy hibiscuses at Gilberg Perennial Farms in Robertsville, Missouri. Photo by Ken Gilberg.

Plate 21. This brilliant red flower resulted from an experimental cross between *Hibiscus moscheutos* and *H. coccineus*. Photo by Ken Gilberg.

Plate 22. Another experimental cross between *Hibiscus moscheutos* and *H. coccineus* gave rise to a plant with handsome, deep pink flowers.

Plate 23. Tropical hibiscuses resulting from experimental hybridizations. These will be evaluated by a number of standards to see if they are worthy of being propagated and introduced to the marketplace.

Plate 24. These as yet unnamed tropical hibiscuses developed at Yoder will also be evaluated.

Plate 25. *Hibiscus cardiophyllus* (heartleaf hibiscus). Photo by George Yatskievych.

Plate 26. *Hibiscus coulteri* (Coulter hibiscus). Photo by George Yatskievych.

Plate 27. *Hibiscus denudatus* (paleface rosemallow). Photo by Kay Yatskievych.

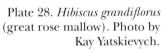

Plate 28. *Hibiscus grandiflorus* (great rose mallow). Photo by Kay Yatskievych.

Plate 29. *Hibiscus laevis* (halberd-leaved rose mallow). Photo by Kay Yatskievych.

Plate 30. Fat flower buds crowd the growing tip of *Hibiscus lasiocarpos* (rose mallow).

Plate 31. *Hibiscus lasiocarpos* (rose mallow).

Plate 32. *Hibiscus schizopetalus* (Japanese lantern).

Plate 33. *Hibiscus syriacus* 'Diana'.

Plate 34. *Hibiscus* 'Blue River II'.

Plate 35. *Hibiscus* 'Everest White'. Photo by Ken Gilberg.

Plate 36. *Hibiscus* 'Lord Baltimore'.

Plate 37. The swirled effect of the petals make the swollen flower bud of *Hibiscus* 'Lord Baltimore' almost as beautiful as the flower. Photo by Ken Gilberg.

Plate 38. *Hibiscus* 'Mauna Kea'.

Plate 39. *Hibiscus* 'Turn of the Century'. Photo by Jack Jennings.

Plate 40. *Hibiscus* 'All Aglow'. Photo by Jack Jennings.

Plate 41. *Hibiscus* 'Amanda Dubin'.

Plate 42. *Hibiscus* 'Blueberry Hill'.

Plate 43. *Hibiscus* 'Byron Metts'.

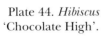

Plate 44. *Hibiscus* 'Chocolate High'.

Plate 45. *Hibiscus* 'Fiesta'.
Photo by Jack Jennings.

Plate 46. *Hibiscus*
'Flaming Wind'.

Plate 47. *Hibiscus* 'Miss Vermont'.

Plate 48. *Hibiscus* 'Texas Rose'.

Plate 49. *Hibiscus* 'Wedding Band'.

Chapter 7

Cultural Problems, Diseases, and Pests

To be a good grower is to be a good detective, able to diagnose and correct plant deficiencies caused by cultural problems, pests, and diseases. It takes some practice to develop these skills. Learning what healthy plants look like is an important first step.

By and large, we have come full circle and now follow gardening methods closer to those practiced prior to World War II, before a wave of pesticides and manufactured fertilizers swept over the earth. Most of us now garden more organically, using few or no pesticides and incorporating natural organic materials into the soil to improve its structure and fertility. We've learned that organic matter not only improves the structure of soil but also inhibits bacterial and fungal diseases by encouraging the growth of mycorrhizal fungi.

As with any other kind of plant, a hibiscus is less vulnerable to pests and diseases if it is healthy. To keep your hibiscus healthy, you must first learn what kinds of conditions exist in its native environment and then try to match those conditions. If you choose a hibiscus that is native to regions similar to yours, or if you are able to match its native conditions within your house or greenhouse, your plant will be much more likely to remain vigorous and healthy.

Integrated Pest Management (IPM) is useful to both home gardeners and commercial growers. It was developed for agricultural purposes and aims to develop a "rifle" approach as an alternative to the "shotgun" technique that has been used for too many years, in which a blanket application of pesticide or fertilizer is used by the calendar rather than by the need. In the past, for example, growers would spray cabbages every two weeks to control cabbage worms. The modern approach involves inspecting the plants and then using a conservative control only if pests are present at an unacceptable level.

IPM consists of several steps. To begin with, identify the pest and learn about its life cycle and natural enemies. Monitor pest populations using observation and traps. Note the extent of injury to plants, and establish a tolerable threshold of injury. Use cultural, biological, and mechanical methods to control unacceptable levels of pest populations with conservative use of the least toxic pesticides only as a last resort. Finally, keep good records and evaluate the effects of your control strategies.

Many conservative pest controls under the IPM umbrella are simple techniques that are easy to follow. For example, many pests can be immediately destroyed either by handpicking them or by dislodging them with a hard spray of cold water. Others can be killed by using parasitic organisms or microbial organisms. Rotating crops is another useful technique, and it is always a good idea to use disease- and pest-resistant varieties. Make sure to destroy diseased plants, and keep a clean and tidy garden. Also maintain healthy, fertile soil that has abundant microbial life.

Like IPM, Plant Health Care (PHC) programs have captured the hearts of growers with their common-sense approach to the culture of crops, whether small or large, both at home and in commercial ventures. Logically enough, PHC has incorporated IPM into its recommendations. This all-encompassing horticultural philosophy calls for taking a larger view and addressing the entire garden rather than just pests and diseases. It is based on the fact that the more vigorous a plant is, the less susceptible it will be to pests and diseases. Plants that are overfertilized or underfertilized are more susceptible to attacks by pests.

To begin with, PHC advises having a complete soil test done, one that analyzes not only major factors (pH, nitrogen, phosphorus, potassium) but also minor elements and percentage of organic matter. This will establish a benchmark for your soil and get you off to a good start. Select strong, vigorously growing plants that are suited to your area, and try to pick varieties that are resistant to pests and diseases. Remove dead, diseased, and injured growth. Do not add diseased plant matter to the compost pile, and make sure to disinfect contaminated tools. Provide enough light, moisture, and nutrients to guarantee good growth. PHC also advises examining your plants regularly for signs and symptoms of pests and diseases, and using the IPM approach for control.

If you apply these programs and philosophies to growing your hibiscuses, you are bound to have plants that are hale, hearty—and beautiful.

Cultural Problems

Most hibiscuses are tough and able to endure a wide range of conditions. Provide the right exposure, water, and nutrients and they should remain healthy. That said, a variety of environmental factors may lead to certain cultural problems.

Chlorosis is a yellowing of the foliage and may be caused by a number of things: disease pathogens and damage from sucking insects, temperatures that are too hot or too cold, too much or too little moisture in the soil, a deficiency of nutrients, or overexposure to systemic pesticides. Yet this yellowing may merely be the natural shedding of old leaves, especially if the yellowing leaves are near the base of stems or branches. It is important to remember that the causes of chlorosis differ from species to species. Overwatering will not cause chlorosis in hardy hibiscuses derived from wetland species, but it may cause leaves of tropical hibiscuses to yellow.

In plants suffering from iron chlorosis, caused by an iron deficiency, leaves turn yellow while the veins remain green. This condition occurs more often in coastal regions and where soils are acid. Check the pH of the soil. It should be in the range of 6.0 to 7.0. If the pH is not in that range, the iron in the soil may be bound up in insoluble salts, making it unavailable to the plant roots. Adding agricultural lime will raise the pH of acid soils. Oftentimes an organic feeding—an application of compost or well-rotted manure scratched into the soil around the base of the plant—will help correct chlorosis, though it may take a while. Changing soil pH is not a speedy process.

Flower bud drop is common in unhealthy hibiscuses. It is often the direct result of inadequate watering, a condition that is especially likely if the plants are being grown in clay containers and the weather is hot and windy. Bud drop may also be due to insect or nematode infestation or to nutritional deficiencies. Some hibiscus experts report that overfertilizing with nitrogen will also cause flower buds to drop. Furthermore, excessive fertilizing with material that is high in nitrogen will result in more foliage and fewer flowers.

Poor flowering may be caused by inadequate light. Hibiscuses require plenty of sun, at least four to six hours, if they are to set plenty of flower buds. Too little sun will also result in sparse foliage. Poor flower production may also be caused by insects or some other factor injuring the flower buds.

Leaf drop can be a natural occurrence as the plant grows and sheds the lower, older leaves near the base of stems or branches. An untimely frost can injure the leaves of tropical and occasionally even hardy hibiscuses, causing leaves to turn brown and drop off. Again, too much or too little water and too much or too little heat can also cause leaf damage and leaf drop. Hot wind can sear the leaves, giving them burned brown edges, especially under droughty conditions. Leaf drop can also be caused by damage to the root system.

An odd condition that may occur with tropical hibiscuses is

that the flowers may change color or form. Flowers may appear as normal during summer and fall, with oddball blooms occurring in the off seasons. Colors may not develop as they should for a given cultivar. Flower form may revert from double to single, from overlapped to plain single, or from ruffled to unruffled. These problems are thought to be due to the many years of inbreeding and backcrossing involved in hybridization: old characteristics that had been thought to have been bred out of a particular strain occasionally reappear.

Diseases

Plant diseases are caused by pathogens of three major types: fungi, bacteria, and viruses. Hibiscus diseases are few, and when they do occur they are usually not life-threatening. That said, hibiscuses should always be monitored and any diseased portions removed and destroyed. Plant diseases require a susceptible host; plants that are damaged or weak are more likely to be affected.

Fungal Diseases

The most common fungal disease of hibiscuses is leaf spot: brown or black spots that appear on foliage, especially in wet weather. In addition, tropical hibiscuses sometimes get root rot, though this may be prevented by good watering practices and prudent use of compost and mulch. Several fungal diseases are known by descriptive, symptomatic names, such as brown rot, canker, damping off, downy mildew, leaf spot, powdery mildew, and rust. Fungicides are preventives only and will not cure these diseases. Learning how to use proper cultural practices will help reduce the likelihood of disease.

Fungal diseases are usually spread by means of the reproductive spores that are carried from one place to another by wind, water, invertebrates, and people. The spores are tough, generally surviving in a dormant state until they land on a receptive host, where they germinate and develop the networks of thread-like mycelium that constitute the main bodies of fungi. This mycelium is what will damage plant roots, by parasitizing the cells.

There are ways to minimize fungal diseases. Plant disease-resistant plants whenever possible. Provide the right kind of environment for the species (always consider sunlight, water, and nutrients). Remove diseased and damaged plant debris from garden beds—fungi are likely to grow in rotting plant matter. Control insects and weeds that are likely to vector or harbor fungal diseases. And remove and destroy any plant parts affected by fungal damage.

Finally, and this is very important, clean and disinfect garden tools regularly, especially if they have been used on infected plants. Also be sure to wash your hands thoroughly if you have been working with diseased plants. A good disinfectant can be made of a dilute solution of 0.5 percent sodium hypochlorite (household bleach), one part bleach to ten parts water, or a solution of 70 percent isopropyl alcohol.

Bacterial Diseases

Bacterial diseases, which rarely affect hibiscuses, are easy to confuse with fungal diseases. Pathogenic bacteria can cause dwarfing, leaf distortion, leaf wilt, stem canker, and stem rot. Different symptoms may affect different parts of the plant. Bacterial diseases may be spread by insect vectors or by splashing water, rain, or fog. Bacteria enter a plant through natural openings such as the stomata. Avoid bacterial diseases in the garden by following the same precautions for fungal diseases.

Viral Diseases

Symptoms of viral disease often include curling, crinkling, puckering, and general distortion of the leaves. Leaf curl caused by insects usually occurs in limited areas. Viral disease can also cause mottling of the leaves and flowers. These diseases are usually specific to their host plants. While there are viral diseases of hibiscuses, they are not common. It is important to note, however, that leaf curl is a symptom of some hibiscus viral diseases.

Viral diseases are not curable, and plants with signs of viral disease should be destroyed. The spread of viral diseases is not completely understood, although it is known that they may be spread by people from plant to plant on tools and hands. For this reason it is important to wash your hands carefully and to sterilize tools after working on plants with questionable symptoms. Insects may serve as vectors. Viral diseases may also be spread when diseased plants are propagated.

Pests

Not many pests bother with the tough foliage of hibiscuses, but some may pose problems. Among the chewing insects that might affect these plants are insect larvae, leaf miners, leaf rollers, cabbage loopers, corn earworms, and sawflies. Beetles, grasshoppers, and katydids may eat the foliage. Certain sucking insects may attack hibiscuses as well, including aphids, leaf hoppers, mealy bugs, scale insects, thrips, and whiteflies. Scale is perhaps the toughest pest to control. Regular close inspection of hibiscus plants is key to preventing a buildup of scale.

The simplest way to get rid of any of these pests is to pick them off hibiscus leaves and flowers or knock them off with a fine hard spray of water. Japanese beetles can be a problem for hardy hibiscuses early in the season when the foliage is tender, but they are usually gone before the summer bloom season. Again, follow the precepts of IPM and PHC for good conservative control of pests.

Deer populations have grown to ridiculous numbers throughout the United States and much of Canada. These large mammals weigh anywhere from 50 to 275 pounds (22.7 to 125 kg) and can decimate a garden in no time. If they are very hungry they will eat just about anything they can chew—it wouldn't surprise me to hear that hungry deer had stripped wood siding off of someone's home. Deer are no longer compared with Bambi. They have become to many, as friends in the East have told me, "rats with antlers." One of the best defenses is to grow plants that deer will not like. Rose of Sharon (*Hibiscus syriacus*) is a shrub that deer seem to abhor. Unfortunately, however, deer seem to be fond of hardy hibiscus flowers. The flowers appear from summer to fall, coinciding with the heaviest period of deer activity, when the young ones are growing and hungry. Deer also thrive on tropical hibiscuses, though in temperate regions these plants are often kept in containers on patios where deer seldom venture. Aside from constructing high fences and using guard dogs, the only defense is to use a deer repellent. Read the directions carefully as with any garden product, and make sure to reapply the product after a rain. Since deer sometimes become used to a repellent, it may be necessary to switch brands every now and then.

In some areas rabbits may also be a problem, but hardy hibiscus flowers are usually out of their reach.

Geese can be a problem near bodies of water. They seem to like browsing on hibiscus flowers. Keep flowering plants above their reach, or use a fence or the family dog to keep them at a distance.

Chapter 8

Propagation

If the goal is to produce clones of the parent plants, propagate hibiscuses asexually by rooted cuttings. If instead the goal is to produce offspring that are genetically different from the parents, cross-pollinate the flowers and raise hybrids from the resulting seeds. Many plant breeders use the latter method of sexual propagation in their pursuit of new cultivars. Others select plants with what they consider to be improved characteristics from seed-grown crops that have been field-pollinated by bees or other pollinating agents. Keep good records if you think you might want to patent or register the resulting plants of any breeding program.

Hibiscus flowers are complete, meaning they have all the possible parts—all four whorls, as the botanists would say: sepal, petal, stamen (filament, anther), and carpal (ovary, style, stigma). To discourage self-pollination and yet have a failsafe method for reproduction, the hibiscus flower has stamens that are positioned below the stigma, making it unlikely that pollen will fall on the stigma of the same flower. Early in the day, the filament and anther of the stamen are positioned to attract insects. Later in the day, the style and stigma curve over to touch pollen-laden anthers, just in case.

In recent years tissue culture, or micropropagation, has become another way to successfully multiply plants. Cells of undifferentiated or meristematic tissue, often from shoot tips, are cultured in vitro (under glass) in sterile conditions on specific nutrient media. When tiny plants develop as the result of this very technical form of asexual reproduction, they are pricked out and planted in tiny pots. Then they are brought along and raised in the same way as seed-grown plants.

Tissue culture allows professional plant breeders to obtain large numbers of clones of new cultivars. The benefit for gardeners is that new cultivars are more quickly available and at lower prices. Since it is a highly technical process requiring special equipment and supplies as well as special training, tissue culture is best left to professionals.

Research scientists at California State University, Fresno, are working on a new high-tech method of creating hibiscus hybrids from sexually incompatible parent species. Rose of Sharon (*Hibiscus syriacus*) and China rose (*H. rosa-sinensis*) have been selected as parents in the hopes that a new plant might have the cold hardiness of the former and the brilliant flowers of the latter. The technique involves isolating cells from each of the two species, breaking down their cell walls, and fusing the cells together with electrical current. This kind of research is part of a new vision for plant breeding. If this particular project is successful, it will result in a hardy landscape plant with new colors for the gardener's palette. In the future we will undoubtedly hear more about this and similar cellular techniques for combining incompatible plants to create varieties with special combinations of characteristics.

Tip Cuttings

One easy way to produce clones is to propagate hibiscuses asexually by tip cuttings. Be sure to select vigorous tips with good color. Water the plants that you will use for tip cuttings thoroughly in the morning. Use sterilized clippers or shears to cut tips at the point about four leaf nodes down where the bark turns from green to brown. Make the cuts at a 45-degree angle so as to expose as much of the undifferentiated tissue (cambium layer) just under the bark as possible.

Remove leaves from the lower half of each cutting and cut away about half of any larger leaves. Dip the cut end into a rooting stimulant. Gently stick the cuttings into pots, trays, or pans of growing medium such as horticultural vermiculite. Don't stick them in too deeply. Keep the medium moist but not soggy. Temperature is important: make sure to keep the medium at 70° to 80°F (21° to 27°C). This is a good reason for taking cuttings during the warmer months. Propping plastic wrap over the containers should help conserve moisture.

The cuttings should be rooted in four to six weeks. A gentle tug on the leaves will tell you if a cutting has rooted. If the cuttings have been in a greenhouse, gradually harden them off before transplanting them in the ground or into individual pots. In order to get bushier plants, plant three to four or even more cuttings per pot, depending on the size of the new pot.

Air Layering

Air layering is another asexual form of propagation. This method, practiced more than two millennia ago by the Chinese, can result in a larger plant in less time than increasing plants from tip shoots. Plan to air layer a plant in warm weather, as rooting will take place more quickly. Make one or two small notches or wide ½-inch (1.25-cm) cuts through the bark of the trunk or stem to be air layered, the exact number depending on the size of the stem. The point is to expose enough undifferentiated cambium tissue for roots to develop.

Fine sphagnum moss should be moistened thoroughly. Squeeze the moss until no more water drips from it and press it around the area to be layered. Cover the moss securely with a layer of plastic (vinyl or polyethylene), then seal the seam and both top and bottom with several winds of waterproof tape. The aim is to seal in the moisture while keeping out rain or other additional moisture. After four or more weeks, when you see roots growing through the sphagnum, remove the wrap and moss, sever the new plant from the parent, and plant it out in the garden or in a pot.

Grafting

Hibiscuses may also be propagated asexually by grafting. This may be a good way to strengthen a weak variety and is also a fast way to increase the number of plants of a specific variety. Grafting is the means used for creating standard hibiscuses. A small, bushy hibiscus is grafted onto a straight, tall hibiscus pruned to look like a miniature tree trunk. This involves taking the scion (a piece of upper growth, a bud or twig) and joining it to the stock (the lower part of a compatible plant, often just a rooted stub).

There are a number of different kinds of grafts, including side grafts, cleft grafts, bud grafts, and tip grafts, but side grafting is the technique most often used by hibiscus growers and hobbyists. You will need a top-quality, sharp knife of carbon steel that will hold an edge.

The American Hibiscus Society recommends cutting a piece of scion wood about 3 inches (7.5 cm) long, one that has at least two leaf buds. Sharpen this to a pointed wedge with one even stroke on each side. Insert the wedge into a cut made in the understock at an angle of about 60 degrees. Match up the cambium layers as much as possible, then bind the graft firmly with grafting tape or polyethylene tape. Pinch off any buds on the stock growing below the graft. Once the graft has grown 2 to 4 inches (5 to 10 cm), cut off the top of the understock and remove the tape.

The flowers, which will appear within a few months, will likely be smaller at first than those of the scion parent, but they will reach full size as the grafted plant matures.

Hybridizing Hibiscuses

Hybridizing, or "pollen daubing," is a form of sexual propagation and is a way to create new plants with different gene combinations. Crossing one plant with desirable characteristics with another that has other desirable characteristics may result in a hybrid that includes some of the best of both parents. It may also, however, result in a plant with no desirable characteristics at all. Plants breeders seek to improve on characteristics such as growth habit and size; flower shape, color, and size; leaf shape and color; and stem color.

Playing the part of the bee is quite simple. You take pollen from the male (pollen parent) and daub it on the receptive stigma of the female (pod parent). Since hibiscuses have complete flowers, they can also be self-pollinated. To do this, put the pollen of a flower onto the stigma of the same flower. Many breeders, especially breeders of the genetically complex *Hibiscus rosa-sinensis*, simply pluck one flower from the pollen parent and smear the pollen-bearing anthers on the stigmas of the chosen pod parent.

Purists who want to be absolutely sure of the parentage of their plants will go to great lengths. When plants are blooming vigorously, begin in the morning by carefully cutting off the petals of an unopened hibiscus bud and removing the anthers. Then bag the entire bud. The next morning, when the stigmas are receptive (usually sticky), remove the bag and pollinate with pollen gathered from ripe anthers of the pollen parent. Bag the flower once again until the stigmas wither, usually in one or two days. Ideally, temperatures should be 60° to 80°F (16° to 27°C). Be sure to label the growing seedpod, which will mature in a few weeks. When the pods are brown and dried, harvest the seeds and store them in a cool dry place until you are ready to sow them.

Hibiscus moscheutos, H. laevis, H. coccineus, H. grandiflorus, H. lasiocarpos, and their many hybrids and cultivars are known collectively as the rose mallows. These native American hardy hibiscuses are similar in chromosomal makeup ($2n - 38$), and modern plant breeders are taking advantage of this fact to develop some wonderful new plants for the garden.

Similarly, breeders of tropical hibiscuses are taking advantage of the great genetic complexity to be found in *Hibiscus rosa-sinensis* to develop varieties with new colors, forms, and textures. This species has a long history and is probably the result of many ancient crosses and hybridizations. It not only offers tremendous hereditary variety but is also genetically compatible with some of the other tropical species, including the exotic *H. schizopetalus.*

Other Means of Altering Plants

Changes in the form or color of a plant's leaves or flowers occasionally occur through natural mutation. Certain techniques that use mutagenic chemicals, ultraviolet light, and irradiation may also cause changes to a plant. These changes may or may not be inheritable.

There are also procedures and techniques for artificially causing the chromosome counts of plants to increase with the use of certain chemicals. Most plants are diploids. Tetraploids can be created with such chemicals as colchicine. Tetraploids are generally sturdier and have more substance than the parent plants. Sometimes the tetraploid conversion is made in order to improve interspecies fertility for the purpose of hybridization. Tetraploids can be so vigorous that they must be reduced to triploids in order to be tamed.

Genetically Compatible Hibiscuses

Some *Hibiscus* species will crossbreed with one another, while others will not. It depends upon how closely related they are.

A number of hardy hibiscuses will cross with each other. According to breeder Harold Winters, those that are compatible include *Hibiscus coccineus, H. grandiflorus, H. laevis, H. lasiocarpos, H. moscheutos,* and *H. mutabilis.* All are native to the eastern United States except *H. mutabilis,* which originated in China.

Ross H. Gast surmised that several tropical hibiscuses are genetically compatible with *Hibiscus rosa-sinensis* and with each another. These include *H. schizopetalus* from the East Africa coastal region and *H. kokio* and *H. arnottianus* from Hawaii. Gast also included several species not listed in modern references; in all likelihood these are misidentified species or forms that have since been incorporated into other species.

Growing Hibiscuses from Seed

With the exception of *Hibiscus rosa-sinensis,* most *Hibiscus* species will grow true to the parental type from seed. Hybrids, of course, will not grow true to the parental type because they have resulted from at least one cross of two genetically different parent plants.

Growing from seed takes more patience than growing from cuttings. You can speed up the germination process by scoring the seeds or soaking them in tepid water overnight, but this is not required. Plant the seeds in commercial flats or other shallow containers with drainage holes. Use a good-quality commercial medium that is formulated for starting seeds. Growers have for many years grown seeds successfully using horticultural vermiculite, but other mediums may work just as well.

A good rule of thumb for most seeds is to plant them at a depth equal to their diameter. Keep the medium moist but not soggy. Placing clear plastic over the container will help conserve moisture; this can be tented to keep it above the tiny plants as they grow. Keep the containers in bright light but not direct sun. It will probably take about three weeks for seedlings to appear.

Once the seedlings have at least two sets of true leaves, you can prick them out and plant them into small pots. At this stage, use a first-rate commercial growing mix. Grow as you would any young plants, gradually introducing the hibiscuses to direct sun. Replant to larger pots as necessary.

Plant Patents

Most new hibiscus cultivars are protected by plant patents. In catalogs these plants appear with labels such as PPAF (plant patent applied for) or PP (plant patent) followed by the patent number. Breeders apply for plant patents to protect their ownership of hybridized or selected varieties of plants that will be asexually reproduced. The patent prevents others from asexually reproducing the plant and selling it. Protection of the plant begins when the patent is issued and continues for twenty years.

Plant patenting was established in May 1930 to provide incentive and protection to plant breeders and horticulturists who originated or discovered any distinct new plant variety that could be asexually reproduced. The first plant patent was issued in August 1931 for the 'New Dawn' rose. By the end of 1988, 6500 plant patents had been granted. In the years since then, thousands more have been granted, including many to cultivars of both tropical and hardy hibiscuses.

The requirements for filing an application are quite simple. First, the plant must have originated as a result of the applicant's efforts—cross-pollination or other breeding efforts, selection of a particular seedling, or selection of a mutation or sport. Second, the plant must not have been introduced to the public or offered for sale to the public for more than one year before filing the application. Finally, the plant must have been asexually reproduced by the applicant.

Anyone can apply for a plant patent. In fact, many hibiscus patents are held by amateur growers. Amateurs, plant breeders, and others who have what they consider to be an outstanding new type of plant may feel free to apply. It would be wise to consult a patent attorney, however, who can prepare and submit the complex proceedings.

Cultivar Records

When compared with botanists, horticulturists have not historically kept very good records, and as a result a lot of information has been lost. Perhaps the practice of patenting cultivars will help with future identifications of the many available varieties, but for now information is sadly lacking as to who bred certain hibiscuses and where and when the process occurred. Plant patents require detailed botanical information and specifics as to the origin.

If I were trying to learn about species instead of cultivars, I could go to the herbarium at the Missouri Botanical Garden and find the voucher sheets for these plants. Each voucher sheet would include a specimen of the plant, including stem, foliage, flower, and seed, as well as pertinent information. Alas, no such records are available for unpatented cultivated plants. As a result I have gone around in circles, by mail, e-mail, and telephone, trying to learn more about the origin of a number of favorite hibiscuses, often going on nothing but anecdotal information. As I learned, the U.S. Patent and Trademark Office can be a good place to learn more about certain plants.

To further fill the gap between botanical and horticultural records, the U.S. National Arboretum has an herbarium that emphasizes plants of horticultural interest. Founded in 1900, it was originally a general herbarium and focused on plants of economic and agricultural interest. In the late 1970s it began to concentrate on collecting specimens of plants of horticultural interest, mainly through contacts with plant breeders. The oldest hibiscus specimen is a sheet of *Hibiscus militaris* (now *H. laevis*) collected on September 13, 1835, from "the north shore of the falls of Ohio" by A. Clapp. In 2003 there were some 600,000 voucher sheets in this herbarium, of which an estimated 200,000 are cultivated plants.

Chapter 9

Botany of Hibiscuses

While it isn't necessary for gardeners to be experienced in botany, there are those who become ever more curious about the plants they are growing. These gardeners want to know where their plants came from and what other plants they are related to. They want to understand the function of the flower parts and learn how the plants reproduce, and they want to know what pollinators work with which plants and whether or not certain plants require pollinators in order to form seeds. Some gardeners may even become interested enough to pursue the field of botany, either formally or informally.

Even if botany is not your favorite subject, I recommend learning a bit about the basic form and structure (morphology) of plants and about general principles of plant classification (taxonomy). A background in science is not necessary to understand these things, and what you learn should prove to be both useful and interesting.

Morphology

Various hibiscuses are called mallows, giant mallows, or rose mallows, and this is because they exhibit many of the botanical attributes found among the mallow family, to which these plants belong. Most hibiscuses in cultivation originated in tropical and subtropical regions, but some are from warm temperate regions. They grow in a wide variety of environments, from swamps and marshes to deserts, savannas, and woodlands.

Hibiscus leaves have petioles and may be simple and entire or lobed or parted (some with lobes cut nearly to the base of the leaf). The alternate leaves usually have palmate veining, and their edges may be smooth, serrate, or scalloped. New leaves are generally covered with fine hairs.

Hibiscus flowers are usually solitary and grow in leaf axils, but they may also appear in clusters or gathered at the upper ends of growth. When they grow in clumps of flowers, the basal bracts are sometimes united and are usually attached at the base of the calyx, depending upon the species. The calyx is composed of five sepals that envelop the base of the petals and form the outer layer of the flower bud, which is usually bell-shaped. The seedpods that develop from the fertilized flowers have five cells corresponding to the five-parted calyx. The small seeds are black.

The five, usually spreading petals are symmetrical, often have dark basal spots of red to maroon, and come in a wide range of colors and color combinations, from white to yellow, pink, red, purplish, or even bluish. Breeders have also developed hibiscuses with semi-double and double flowers. Petals may or may not overlap, depending on the species and variety.

The single most distinguishing feature of the hibiscus flower is the staminal column. The stamens, with numerous pollen-bearing anthers, are united in a tubular column that rises at the center of the flower and that may be longer or shorter than the petals. This column surrounds the style, which usually has five branches at the top but which may only have five lobes.

The style ends in five stigma pads, botanically known as capitate stigmas. In breeding hibiscuses, the pollen from the male parent is placed on the stigma pads of the female parent. These pads are usually sticky when they are mature and ready to receive the pollen. The anthers will split open (dehisce) when the pollen is ripe.

Taxonomy

Botanists have pondered over the taxonomy of the Malvaceae for many years and continue to do so. The one thing they all appear to agree on is that major changes are needed in the classification of this family in order to accommodate new knowledge of its evolutionary history. As DNA studies continue, the results are bringing new light to the relationships in this interesting group.

The genus *Hibiscus* has been and remains an unusually heterogeneous group of plants, so much so that the best distinguishing features are the five stigma pads atop the staminal column and the five-celled capsule or seedpod. These features are found in all species of the genus.

The chromosome numbers of *Hibiscus* species are extremely variable, a factor that, when added to the variety of the specific morphology of the plants, may lead some botanists to further separate disparate groups from the genus.

The genus was named by Linnaeus and first mentioned in 1737 in his *Genera Plantarum*. He later substantiated *Hibiscus* when he included it in his *Species Plantarum* (1753), the monumental book that established the binomial system of naming plants and animals. *Species Plantarum* included twenty species in the genus, nine of which have since been moved to other genera. The remaining species include favorites that are now widely bred and cultivated: rose mallow (*H. moscheutos*), including the white to pink subspecies *moscheutos* and the white subspecies *palustris*; rose of Sharon (*H. syriacus*); and China rose (*H. rosa-sinensis*). Roselle (*H. sabdariffa*) and flower-of-an-hour (*H. trionum*) are also mentioned.

According to botanist David M. Bates, the cultivated species of *Hibiscus* are best managed taxonomically by dividing the genus into several sections. Bates dealt with all the species that were grown horticulturally and offered commercially in the United States during the 1940s, 1950s, and early 1960s.

In the 1988 publication *Malvaceae of Mexico*, Paul Fryxell organized the plants of this family into sections, following the lead of Bénédict P. G. Hochreutiner, who had subdivided the genus *Hibiscus* into botanical sections in 1900.

Bates, Fryxell, and others in botany agreed that several of the larger genera of Malvaceae were taxonomic challenges, with the genus *Hibiscus* being the most difficult. Fryxell said in 2002 (personal communication), "It is my belief that *Hibiscus* must be handled differently than the other large genera of the Malvaceae, because it presents a different set of problems, and that further fragmentation of *Hibiscus*, although it may ultimately be warranted, is premature."

Many other botanists have been involved in the study of *Hibiscus*. Botanical sleuthing continues, with the most active work being carried out by Australian botanists Curt Brubaker, Lyn Craven, and Bernard Pfeil. Working under the umbrella of the Centre for Plant Biodiversity Research, they are collaborating with others in Australia and the United States in their studies of evolutionary relationships in the Malvaceae, paying special attention to the genus *Hibiscus*. Molecular studies currently underway will probably result in changes to the relationships among the sections and species of *Hibiscus*.

I was surprised to find that the cultivated species and varieties of *Hibiscus* have not yet been sorted out taxonomically. It seems that in botany as in other sciences, there are mountains of knowledge still to be climbed. Further DNA and molecular studies will be needed to figure out exactly what is what in this interesting group of ornamentals.

Chapter 10

A Gallery of Hibiscuses

Of the roughly 220 species in the genus *Hibiscus*, a bit more than three dozen are commonly grown. This may not sound like many, but when you add in the cultivars, this genus begins to seem like an endless parade of showy plants. The hibiscuses listed in this chapter are among the best-known and most commonly cultivated plants of the Malvaceae. Species are listed first, followed by rose of Sharon cultivars, hardy hibiscus cultivars, and tropical hibiscus cultivars.

The species descriptions include definitions of specific epithets, which besides providing useful background information are also interesting in and of themselves. Many species are named in honor of a person, such as the discoverer of the plant. Some names describe the origin of a plant, or a characteristic feature. In a few cases where the origin of a species name was extremely obscure I have had to guess at a definition.

It is often hard to know the exact parentage of hibiscus cultivars, since breeding records are frequently lacking. Many hardy hibiscus cultivars include *Hibiscus moscheutos* in their genetic history, but *H. coccineus*, *H. grandiflorus*, *H. laevis*, and *H. lasiocarpos* may also be parent species. Most tropical hibiscuses found in nurseries, florists, and plant centers are descended from *H. rosa-sinensis*, but again, parentage is sometimes unclear. Names of breeders or propagators, where known, are placed parenthetically at the ends of cultivar descriptions.

Hibiscus Species

Hibiscus acetosella. The species name means "slightly acid." This woody perennial, known as cranberry hibiscus, must be treated as an annual in cooler regions. The leaves often have a reddish tint and are usually glabrous, though they sometimes have a fine blush of stiff hairs. Leaves vary from entire to having three or five lobes. The single flowers grow in leaf axils and are either yellow or reddish purple with a dark purple base. Plants grow to a height of 5 feet (1.5 m). Native to eastern and central Africa. Zone 10.

Hibiscus aculeatus. The species name means "with prickles" or "thorny" and refers to the few spines on the stems and petioles. This annual plant, known as comfort root, pineland hibiscus, or big thicket hibiscus, is sturdy and large-textured. Some refer to it as "okra on steroids." The cream to yellow, 8-inch (20-cm) flowers are favorites of hummingbirds. The flower petals are notched as if cut with pinking shears. The leaves are more narrow and somewhat rougher than those of most hibiscuses. The bloom season is from June through October. This plant will thrive if grown in soil that is well-draining, moist, and acidic. It grows in savannas, ditches, roadsides, and pinewoods. Native from Texas to the Carolinas in the southern tier of each state. Zone 10.

Hibiscus ×archeri. This hybrid was named in honor of William Archer (1820–1874), an Australian correspondent of Joseph D. Hooker, one of the first directors of England's Royal Botanic Gardens, Kew. It appears to have resulted from an unplanned garden hybridization (*H. rosa-sinensis × H. schizopetalus*). It is very much like *H. rosa-sinensis* except that its branching is more delicate and its leaves more coarsely serrate. The petals of the usually red flowers range from crenate or scalloped to having narrow, finely cut lobes. Zone 9.

Hibiscus arnottianus. The specific epithet refers to George Arnott Walker Arnott (1799–1868), Scottish botanist, professor, traveler, collector, and director of the Glasgow Botanic Gardens. The common name is Wilder's white. In Hawaii, where the species is native, it is called koki'o, which is also a common name for *H. kokio.* This plant grows to about 30 feet (9 m) tall as a shrub or small tree. The ovate, entire to dentate leaves are 6 to 10 inches (15 to 25 cm) long, dark green, and leathery. Solitary flowers are slightly fragrant, 4 inches (10 cm) or more in diameter, and pure white to white with pale pink veins. Flowers also have red filaments. The staminal column is exerted from the corolla. Zone 10.

Hibiscus brackenridgei. The species name refers to William Dunlop Brackenridge (1810–1893), Scottish American horticulturist and superintendent of the National Botanic Garden in Washington, D.C. This shrub to small tree may be erect or sprawling, reaching anywhere from 10 to 30 feet (3 to 9 m) tall. Leaves, up to 6 inches (15 cm) across, are three-, five-, or seven-lobed and coarsely serrate. Yellow to red flowers, often with a maroon base, are solitary or in racemes and about 7 inches (17.5 cm) in diameter. The staminal column is exerted. Native to Hawaii. Zone 10.

Hibiscus cameronii. This species was named in honor of David Cameron, curator of the Birmingham Horticultural Society, England, during the 1830s. It is also known as pink hibiscus. The cup-shaped flowers are 3 to 4 inches (7.5 to 10 cm) in diameter, have prominent veining, and are rich pink with red-purple or deep rose at the base of the petals. The staminal column is bright red, exerted, and curved downward. Leaves are less commonly entire but most often lobed with three, five, or seven lobes that go halfway to the base of the leaves. This plant grows 3 to 6 feet (0.9 to 1.8 m) tall. Native to Madagascar. Zone 10.

· *Hibiscus cannabinus.* The specific epithet means "hemp-like." Known widely as kenaf, this species probably originated in the East Indies but is now considered native to east-central Africa. It has been widely introduced in Mexico, Cuba, Egypt, Thailand, Russia, and China, where it used to manufacture paper, roping, and other fiber products. This prickly-stemmed annual or short-lived perennial grows up to 15 feet (4.5 m) tall and has three- to seven-lobed palmate leaves up to 6 inches (15 cm) long. Kenaf usually has a single stem and an erect pattern of growth. The summer to autumn flowers that grow in the leaf axils are bell-shaped and usually yellow, more rarely purplish. Flowers have crimson to purple-red centers and grow either singly or in racemes of a few flowers each. Zone 10.

Hibiscus cardiophyllus (Plate 25). The species name refers to this plant's cordate leaves. Commonly called heartleaf hibiscus or tulipan del monte, this evergreen perennial is tolerant of hot, arid conditions and salt air. It is native to the Coastal Bend area of Texas and grows well in full to partial sun in gravelly, well-draining soil. Mature plants reach 2 to 3 feet (0.6 to 0.9 m) tall and about 2 feet (0.6 m) wide. The large, showy, red to orange-red flowers are 2½ inches (6.75 cm) in diameter and appear from spring to fall. The flowers attract both butterflies and humming-birds. The bark is smooth and greenish brown with numerous tiny white elongated spots. Propagation can be by fresh seed or by softwood cuttings. Zones 8 to 11.

Hibiscus cisplatinus. The specific epithet refers to the Rio de La Plata, a large estuary southeast of Buenos Aires, where this plant was originally discovered. This South American plant, native to Argentina, Paraguay, and southern Brazil, is commonly grown as a shrub in Hawaii. Its stems grow up to 8 feet (2.4 m) tall and

Hibiscus cameronii (Knowles et al. 1837–1840). Courtesy of the
Missouri Botanical Garden Library.

Hibiscus cannabinus (Cavanilles 1785–1787). Courtesy of the Missouri Botanical Garden Library.

have coarse yellow spines. Three- or five-lobed palmate leaves are up to 6 inches (15 cm) long. Bell-shaped, rose-colored flowers with a purplish eye are 4 to 6 inches (10 to 15 cm) in diameter and grow in upper leaf axils. Zone 10.

Hibiscus coccineus. The species name means "red." Known as swamp hibiscus or red water hibiscus, this plant is native to the southeastern United States from Florida to Georgia, where it grows in damp or wet sites. It usually grows to about 6 feet (1.8 m) tall, though some specimens may reach up to 10 feet (3 m). The deep red summer flowers, up to 6 inches (15 cm) in diameter, grow in upper leaf axils and have the typical exerted staminal column. The three-, five-, or seven-lobed leaves, up to 8 inches (20 cm) wide, are smooth, glaucous, and somewhat reminiscent of Japanese maple leaves. Many plants of this species have a reddish look to the green foliage and may have more than a hint of red in the stems as well. Cultivars are this species are quite beautiful, often with flowers the size of dinner plates. Zone 6.

Hibiscus coulteri (Plate 26). This species was named in honor of Irish botanist Thomas Coulter (1793–1843), who worked in Mexico for the Real del Monte Mining Company and later in California and Arizona. Although Coulter collected the species in northern Mexico, it was another botanist, Charles Wright, who prepared the type specimen and named the plant. This shrubby hibiscus, called Coulter hibiscus or desert rosemallow, grows in brushy canyons and desert hills from western Texas to southern Arizona and northern Mexico. It often reaches up to 4 feet (1.2 m) tall. Lower leaves are entire, while upper leaves are divided into three narrow lobes that are serrate. Cup-shaped flowers are large, 1 to 2 inches (2.5 to 5 cm) across, and yellow to pale yellowish white, often with a red to maroon eye. Flowering occurs from April through August, or throughout the year in warm climates. Zones 8 to 10.

Hibiscus denudatus (Plate 27). The species name means "denuded" or "stripped" and may refer to the greatly reduced or often absent involucre. Known by a number of common names, including paleface rosemallow, desert hibiscus, rock rose mallow, and naked hibiscus, this subshrub grows 1 to 3 feet (0.3 to 0.9 m) tall. It is native to rocky slopes and canyons from Texas, Colorado, Nevada, southern California, and south to central Mexico. The foliage is densely covered with yellowish wool, and the leaf blades are finely dentate and ovate, up to 1.25 inches (3 cm) long. The white to pinkish to lavender flowers, small for this genus, appear during the warm season and grow on short stems in upper axils. The petals are often reddish at the base. Zones 7 to 10.

Hibiscus coccineus (*The Garden* 1874). Courtesy of the Missouri Botanical Garden Library.

Hibiscus diversifolius. The species name refers to the variability of the leaves. This small shrub grows to a height of about 3 feet (0.9 m), with prickly stems and hairy, palmate, five-lobed leaves. Pale yellow 4-inch (10-cm) flowers have a maroon center and are more cupped and less flat than the typical hibiscus flower. This plant originated in tropical Africa and Asia but has been introduced into Central and South America. Like many of the American natives of southeastern states, this species will tolerate damp or even soggy soils. Zone 10.

Hibiscus elatus. The specific epithet means "tall" or "high." This species, often called Cuban bast or mahoe, is native to Cuba and Jamaica, where its fibrous inner bark has been used for many years to wrap cigars. The flowers are about 6 inches (15 cm) in diameter and orange-yellow to orange-red fading to deep crimson. The petals are not overlapping. Zone 10.

Hibiscus furcellatus. The species name means "diminutively forked." Its common names are rose hibiscus and lindenleaf hibiscus. This is a weedy hibiscus with lavender to maroon flowers and prickly branches. Flowers are about 7 inches (17.5 cm) in diameter. Native to Central and South America, the West Indies, and parts of the United States (Florida, Hawaii). Zone 10.

Hibiscus fuscus. The species name means "bright brown" or "swarthy." This shrub grows up to 10 feet (3 m) tall. It is native from Ethiopia to South Africa and westward to the Congo, where it grows at the edges of savannas and forests. The flowers are small for a hibiscus, only about 2 inches (5 cm) in diameter. These are yellow to white with orange anthers and grow in clusters at the ends of branches. Zone 10.

Hibiscus grandiflorus (Plate 28). The species name means "large-flowered." Called the great rose mallow or velvet mallow, this native of the southeastern United States is often confused with *H. moscheutos* but can be distinguished by its leaves, which are broader than they are long and deeply lobed with three or five parts. The 5- to 6-inch (12.5- to 15-cm) flowers may be pink, white, or rose-purple and sometimes have a crimson spot at the base of each petal. Some sources believe that this is not a species but rather a hybrid selection of crosses between *H. moscheutos* and similar North American hibiscuses. There are many beautiful cultivars, some with flowers 12 inches (30 cm) in diameter. Zone 8.

Hibiscus hamabo. The specific epithet derives from the Japanese *hama*, meaning "beach." Plants sold under this name are often actually selections of *H. syriacus*, with single pink or pinkish lavender flowers that have a crimson spot at the base of each petal. This branching shrub grows up to about 15 feet (4.5 m) tall. Leaves are elliptical to oval, minutely toothed, spiny at the tip, and 3 inches (7.5 cm) long. Native to the warmer regions of Japan and Korea. Zone 10.

Hibiscus hastatus. The species name means "spear-shaped." The leaves are three-lobed, with the central lobe approximately twice as long as the other two. Flowers nearly 6 inches (15 cm) in diameter grow in clusters at the ends of branches and have overlapping petals. Newly opened flowers are white to yellow, usually with a brownish red to red center. As the flowers age, the petals and staminal columns fade from orange to deep red. This shrub to small tree is native to the Society Islands, a group of islands in the South Pacific that comprise part of French Polynesia. Zone 10.

Hibiscus heterophyllus. The species name means "diversely leaved." The leaves of this evergreen shrub are oval or elliptical, sometimes with three deep lobes, and are sometimes narrow and obovate near the top of the plant. Flowers are pink, yellow, or white with a pink margin and may have thin striping or purple-red

Hibiscus hamabo (Dippel 1889–1893). Courtesy of the Missouri Botanical Garden Library.

basal spots. Native to warm regions of northern Australia, especially New South Wales and Queensland. Zone 10.

Hibiscus indicus. The specific epithet means "from India," though the species seems to have originated in southern China. This shrub to small tree grows up to about 10 feet (3 m) tall. The palmate leaves have three, five, or seven lobes and are 6 inches (15 cm) long. Single or rarely double flowers are 4 to 6 inches (10 to 15 cm) in diameter and white when first open, gradually turning pink, then red. This species is similar to *H. mutabilis,* and the two are often confused. The differences, notably in the seedpods, are unlikely to be noticed by the average person. Zone 10.

Hibiscus kokio. The specific epithet, which derives from the Hawaiian word for "shaggy" or "woolly," can cause confusion, since *H.*

arnottianus is commonly called koki'o. This red-flowered native of Hawaii, known as red hibiscus, grows up to 20 feet (6 m) tall. The 3- to 4-inch (7.5- to 10-cm) flowers are orange-red to red, more rarely orange or yellow, sometimes with a red basal spot. One unusual characteristic of the flowers is that the filaments are reflexed. This plant's characteristics vary from location to location. The more attractive forms have been used in crossings with *H. rosa-sinensis*. This species is listed as an endangered plant. Zone 10.

Hibiscus laevis (Plate 29). The species name of the synonym, *H. militaris*, refers to the spear-like shape of the leaves, and common names for this hibiscus include halberd-leaved rose mallow and soldier rose mallow. *Laevis* means "smooth," in reference to the glabrous nature of the stems and foliage. This species is native from southern Pennsylvania to southern Minnesota and in much of the southeastern United States. It grows 6 to 7 feet (1.8 to 2.1 m) tall. The summer flowers, up to 6 inches (15 cm) in diameter, are off-white to pale pink with a dark red eye. The cultivars of this hibiscus are stunning, often with huge flowers. Zone 6.

Hibiscus lasiocarpos (Plates 30 and 31). The species name means "hairy-seeded" or "furry-seeded." This plant, known as rose mallow, grows up to 6 feet (1.8 m) tall. Its 4- to 6-inch (10- to 15-cm) flowers are white or rose with a magenta to crimson eye. The leaves are very hairy, ovate to lanceolate, and 4 to 7 inches (10 to 17.5 cm) long. Native to the United States, this plant of damp and wet areas is found growing wild from southern Missouri and Illinois to Florida, Texas, and eastern New Mexico. Oddly, this species is also found in central California and Mexico. This species often grows in large showy colonies. Zones 5 to 6.

Hibiscus lavaterioides. The epithet is a tip of the hat to the Lavater brothers, Swiss physicians and naturalists of the seventeenth century. The 5- to 9-inch (12.5- to 22.5-cm) flowers of this shrubby

Hibiscus laevis (Scopoli 1786–1788). Courtesy of the Missouri
Botanical Garden Library.

Hibiscus lasiocarpos (*Garden and Forest* 1888). Courtesy of the Missouri Botanical Garden Library.

plant are pink or lavender and often have white veins. The stigmas are red. The densely pubescent leaves are ovate to cordate
or may be slightly three-lobed. Leaves are 4 to 7 inches (10 to
17.5 cm) long. This plant is native to Central America, Mexico,
and the West Indies. Zone 10.

Hibiscus ludwigii. The specific epithet honors the German bota-
nist-physician Christian Gottlieb Ludwig (1709–1773). This 10-
foot (3-m) shrub has epicalyx segments that are broadest at the
base, distinguishing them from similar *Hibiscus* species. Flowers
are 4 inches (10 cm) in diameter and yellow, usually with a
brownish or brownish red eye. Leaves are three- or five-lobed and
4 to 5 inches (10 to 12.5 cm) long. This species grows wild in
Africa from Ethiopia to South Africa. Zone 10.

Hibiscus macrophyllus. The species name means "large-leaved,"
and this plant is called large-leaved hau where it is native, from
India through the Malay Peninsula to Java. It has naturalized in
Hawaii. The circular cordate leaves are indeed large, 8 to 24
inches (20 to 60 cm) in diameter. Flowers are about 4 to 5 inches
(10 to 12.5 cm) in diameter and yellow with purple-red basal
spots. Zone 10.

Hibiscus moscheutos. The species name means "mallow rose," and
this plant is known as the swamp rose mallow or common rose
mallow. It is probably the best-known and is certainly the most
widely found native of North America. In the United States it is
found growing in marshy areas, swamps, and ditches from
Florida to New York, as far west as Texas and Kansas, and in California. The 3- to 9-inch (7.5- to 22.5-cm) leaves are lanceolate to
broadly ovate and may be either unlobed or shallowly lobed in
three or five parts. Leaf edges may be dentate or scalloped. The
white, pink, or rose flowers are 6 to 8 inches (15 to 20 cm) across,
with red bands at the base of the petals. The plant may grow up
to 8 feet (2.4 m) tall. When hybridized this hibiscus produces

very attractive cultivars, some with flowers 12 inches (30 cm) in diameter. Subspecies *moscheutos* has white, sometimes pink, petals that are red at the base. Subspecies *palustris*, the white form, is found more rarely than the pink to red form. It is also being used extensively in hybridizing programs for hardy hibiscuses. Both the species and subspecies are hardy to Zone 5.

Hibiscus mutabilis. The specific epithet, meaning "to mutate or change," refers to the way in which the flowers change color as the day progresses. The 4- to 6-inch (10- to 15-cm) flowers, usually single but sometimes double, are white when they first open but gradually turn pink or red as they age. Forms with double white flowers and forms with double pink flowers have been selected, as has a form with double white flowers that turn to pink. Commonly known as the Confederate rose, cotton rose, or, in China, as tree lotus, this species has long been cultivated in the United States. It grows as a shrub or small tree up to 10 feet (3 m) tall. Native to southern China. Zone 8.

Hibiscus paramutabilis. The specific epithet refers to the way in which the flowers darken as they age. This species is very similar to *H. mutabilis* but can be distinguished by the flower's epicalyx and by the fruit structure. As with *H. mutabilis*, the flower petals of this hibiscus open white or pale-pink and gradually darken throughout the day to pink or rose-pink. This shrub or small tree grows up to 15 feet (4.5 m) tall. Native to eastern China. Zone 9.

Hibiscus pedunculatus. The species name refers to the way the flower is supported on a distinct stalk or stem. This herbaceous perennial or subshrub reaches nearly 7 feet (2.1 m) tall. The 2- to 4-inch (5- to 10-cm) flowers are pale lilac to pale rose-purple. Leaves are usually three-lobed. Native from Mozambique to South Africa. Zone 10.

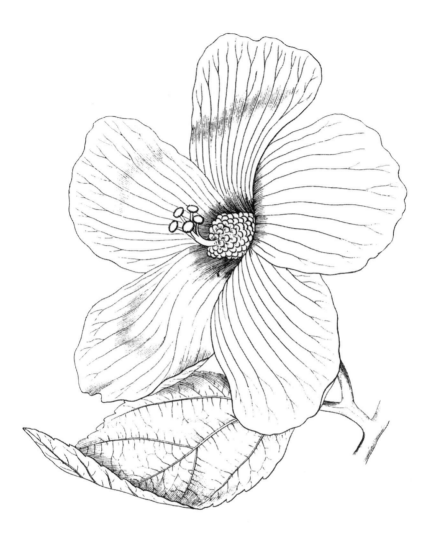

Hibiscus moscheutos (Gray and Sprague 1849). Courtesy of the
Missouri Botanical Garden Library.

Hibiscus mutabilis (Rumpf 1741–1750). Courtesy of the Missouri Botanical Garden Library.

Hibiscus pedunculatus (Cavanilles 1785–1787). Courtesy of the
Missouri Botanical Garden Library.

Hibiscus platanifolius. The species name means "plane tree," in reference to the broad and ample flat leaves. This shrub to small tree grows up to 15 feet (4.5 m) tall. Each white flower petal has a crimson base and is about 3 to 5 inches (7.5 to 12.5 cm) in diameter. Leaves are usually three-lobed. Native to India. Zone 10.

Hibiscus radiatus. The specific epithet means "radiating outward." This plant is very similar to *H. cannabinus* except that its leaves lack the glands found in the latter species. The yellow flowers are marked by a purple center and reach nearly 6 inches (15 cm) in diameter. Leaves are coarsely dentate, and upper leaves are deeply lobed with three or five parts. This species is native to southern and southeastern Asia, where it is often cultivated as a vegetable or as a medicinal herb. Zone 10.

Hibiscus rosa-sinensis. The species name means "China rose," which is also a common name. This species is also known as bunga raya, Chinese hibiscus, Chinese rose, Hawaiian hibiscus, queen of the tropics, rose of China, and shoe black. The leaves are a rich glossy green, dentate, and ovate to broadly lanceolate. Flowers are every color but blue. Although it has been cultured into 1- to 2-foot (0.3- to 0.6-m) potted plants, this hibiscus wants to be a tree. It grows up to 15 feet (4.5 m) tall in tropical and subtropical gardens as well as in places like the Missouri Botanical Garden's Climatron. Although dwarf forms have been bred, the original form has to be pruned regularly if it is not to outgrow its bounds. Botanists believe this species originated somewhere in tropical Asia, but its true origin is lost in history. There are thousands of cultivars, with more being developed each year. Zone 9.

Hibiscus sabdariffa. The epithet is an old Turkish name referring to the redness of this hibiscus and to the acidic flavor of its fleshy calyxes, which are used to make tart jellies, sour drinks, and the

Hibiscus radiatus, from plants collected in 1770 (Banks et al. 1900–1905). Courtesy of the Missouri Botanical Garden Library.

Hibiscus rosa-sinensis (Rumpf 1741–1750). Courtesy of the Missouri Botanical Garden Library.

like. The name may also refer to sand and thus to the fact that this plant thrives in the sandy soil and dry climate of the sub-Saharan region of Africa. Common names include Florida cranberry, roselle, sorrel, Indian sorrel, Jamaica sorrel, and red sorrel. This plant is an annual and a short-day plant, making it difficult to grow in temperate gardens. Leaves may be entire and ovate or palmate with three or five lobes. The 2-inch (5-cm) flowers are pale yellow with purplish red at the base of each petal. This plant grows up to 8 feet (2.4 m) tall. It originated in the Old World tropics and is widely cultivated in subtropical and tropical regions. Zone 10.

Hibiscus schizopetalus (Plate 32). The species name, meaning "divided petals," refers to the finely dissected petals of this unusual hibiscus. Known as fringed hibiscus, Japanese hibiscus, and Japanese lantern, it has pink or red flowers with long slender staminal columns that extend well beyond the petals. The 2½-inch (6.25-cm) petals are deeply recurved and deeply lobed. The ovate, dentate leaves are 3 to 6 inches (7.5 to 15 cm) long. A number of taxonomists believe this species is a selection of *H. rosasinensis* or is at least very closely related. This is another hibiscus that wants to be a tree. It grows up to 15 feet (4.5 m) tall in the wild or in the greenhouse. An African native, it is found in Kenya, northern Mozambique, and Tanzania. Zone 10.

Hibiscus scottii. This species was named in honor of Robert Scott (1757–1808), Irish botanist, physician, plant collector, and professor at Dublin's Trinity College. The 4-inch (10-cm) flowers may grow singly or in twos and threes. Golden yellow flowers are bright red at the base of the petals. The staminal column is pale yellow with crimson stigma pads. Leaves are 4 inches (10 cm) long and may be entire or palmately three-lobed. This shrub to small tree is native to the Yemeni island of Socotra, located in the Indian Ocean near the Horn of Africa. Zone 10.

Hibiscus sabdariffa (Bućhoz 1775–1778). Courtesy of the Missouri
Botanical Garden Library.

Hibiscus schizopetalus (*Gardeners' Chronicle* 1844). Courtesy of the
Missouri Botanical Garden Library.

Hibiscus scottii (Balfour 1888). Courtesy of the Missouri Botanical Garden Library.

Hibiscus sinosyriacus. The specific epithet appears to refer to the Syrian and Chinese origin of this 8-foot (2.4-m) deciduous shrub. Summer to autumn flowers are 3 inches (7.5 cm) in diameter and white, with red centers and white stamens bearing yellow anthers. There is some discrepancy among hibiscus experts as to whether or not this species is actually in cultivation. Some say that the plant sold under this name is in fact *H. paramutabilis.* According to the *Index of Garden Plants* (Griffiths 1994), this species is native to central China and similar to *H. syriacus* but with larger leaves. Zone 8.

Hibiscus syriacus. See chapter 4.

Hibiscus trionum. The specific epithet, meaning "three-colored," refers to the flowers, which are creamy white to pale yellow with yellow stamens and a purple throat. These annuals or short-lived perennials grow up to 6 feet (1.8 m) tall. Known as flower-of-an-hour or bladder ketmia, they are hairy, erect or ascending plants with three- or, less commonly, five-lobed leaves. Native to arid, tropical regions of the Old World. Zone 10.

Hibiscus uncinellus. The species name means "aculeate," in reference to the spines and hooks with which this plant climbs onto other shrubs and trees. It grows to 10 feet (3 m) tall as a shrub, and its climbing branches may grow by as much as 30 feet (9 m). It has three-lobed leaves and lavender flowers. This hibiscus is native to southern Mexico, where it is known as tulipán. It seems to be less well known than many other North American hibiscuses. Zone 10.

Hibiscus waimeae. The specific epithet refers to this plant's origins in the Hawaiian Islands. *Waimea* is a place-name on three or more of the major islands; it comes from *wai* (water) and *mea* (reddish). The extremely fragrant flowers of this plant are solitary, growing at the ends of branches. As they open in the morn-

Hibiscus trionum (Cavanilles 1785–1787). Courtesy of the Missouri Botanical Garden Library.

ing they are white, but in the afternoon they fade to pink. The exerted staminal column is bright red at its tip. The leaves are rounded to broadly ovate-elliptic and 2 to 7 inches (5 to 17.5 cm) long. This species grows as a tree, reaching up to 30 feet (9 m) tall. Zone 10.

Rose of Sharon Cultivars

Hibiscus syriacus 'Admiral Dewey'. Abundant double flowers are
    pure white.

Hibiscus waimeae (Geological and Natural History Survey of Minnesota 1897). Courtesy of the Missouri Botanical Garden Library.

Hibiscus syriacus 'Aphrodite'. Single flowers are mauve with a dark magenta eye. (Egolf)

Hibiscus syriacus 'Ardens'. A plant valued for its broad habit of growth and dense semi-double blue flowers tinged with purple. The lilac centers fade to blue toward the edges.

Hibiscus syriacus 'Blue Bird'. An erect plant featuring large, wide, pale blue flowers with a red eye. (Egolf)

Hibiscus syriacus Blue Satin ('Marina'). A Dutch introduction similar to 'Blue Bird' but with stronger growth. Large single flowers are a richer, deeper shade of blue than any other hibiscus. Winner of an Award of Recommendation from the Royal Boskoop Horticulture Society. (Verweij)

Hibiscus syriacus Blush Satin ('Mathilda'). Very showy, large, blush-pink flowers feature a prominent red eye. Winner of an Award of Recommendation from the Royal Boskoop Horticulture Society. (Verweij)

Hibiscus syriacus 'Boule de Feu'. Named before 1846. Carnation-like double flowers are purple-red with a red eye.

Hibiscus syriacus 'Coelestis'. Named before 1887. Single flowers are pale purple with a rosy hue at the base. Streaks of color reach halfway to the ends of petals.

Hibiscus syriacus 'Diana' (Plate 33). An unusually prolific bloomer, with flowers that remain open for more than a day. Profuse, single, snow-white flowers have waxy petals that are heavily ruffled at the edges. The dark green foliage is also of a heavy texture. Growth habit is erect. Winner of the Royal Horticultural Society Award of Merit and the Pennsylvania Horticultural Society Gold Medal Plant Award. (Egolf)

Hibiscus syriacus 'Duc de Brabant'. Profuse double flowers are deep rose-purple.

Hibiscus syriacus 'Freedom'. A strong plant with profuse, double, dusky dark pink flowers. (Shadow)

Hibiscus syriacus 'Hamabo'. Single flowers are light pink accented with a crimson eye and crimson markings. Reddish stripes go halfway to petal ends. Winner of a Royal Horticultural Society Award of Merit.

Hibiscus syriacus 'Helene'. Abundant single flowers are large, heavily ruffled, and white with a dark red center and red veining. Growth habit is upright. (Egolf)

Hibiscus syriacus 'Hillis Variegated'. A plant noted for its variegated green and gold leaves and semi-double pale pink flowers. Flower buds are candy-striped. Good flower production throughout the summer. Leaves are glabrous and mostly three-lobed with rounded notches. (Hillis)

Hibiscus syriacus 'Jeanne d'Arc'. Semi-double white flowers are tinted a pale pink at the base.

Hibiscus syriacus 'Lady Stanley' (also known as 'Elegantissimus' and 'Bicolor'). Semi-double white flowers have blush-pink sections and red lines that reach halfway to the petal ends. Very similar to 'Leopoldii'.

Hibiscus syriacus Lavender Chiffon ('Notwoodone'). A strong grower. Anemone-like, pale lavender flowers exhibit a puff of stamenoid petals in the center. Winner of a Gold Medal from the Royal Boskoop Horticulture Society. (Woods)

Hibiscus syriacus 'Leopoldii'. Semi-double flowers have blush-pink sections and red lines that reach halfway to the petal ends. Nearly identical to 'Lady Stanley'.

Hibiscus syriacus 'Lucy'. Double flowers are magenta with a rose-red center.

Hibiscus syriacus 'Meehanii'. A low-growing plant with variegated foliage of green with irregular cream-white, yellow, or gray edges. Flowers are mauve with a maroon eye.

Hibiscus syriacus 'Minerva'. Ruffled flowers are violet with a purple-red eye. (Egolf)

Hibiscus syriacus 'Monstrosus'. Named in 1873. Single flowers are white with a maroon eye.

Hibiscus syriacus 'Oiseau Bleu'. First introduced in France in 1958. May be synonymous with 'Blue Bird'. Flowers are blue with a red eye. Winner of a Royal Horticultural Society Award of Merit.

Hibiscus syriacus 'Purpureus Variegatus'. Variegated leaves are green with wide white, yellow, or gray edges. Flowers are dark purple to maroon and never completely open, giving them a mysterious look.

Hibiscus syriacus Rose Satin ('Minrosa'). Large, single, deep rose-pink flowers grow on vigorous plants. (Bellion)

Hibiscus syriacus 'Snowdrift'. Named prior to 1911 and described as an improved form of 'Totus Albus'. Single flowers are pure white.

Hibiscus syriacus 'Snow Storm'. Identical to 'Totus Albus'.

Hibiscus syriacus 'Totus Albus'. Introduced in 1855. Single flowers are pure white.

Hibiscus syriacus 'Violet Claire Double' (also known as 'Violaceus Plenus' and 'Puniceus Plenus'). Semi-double flowers are pale purple with a red-purple center.

Hibiscus syriacus Violet Satin ('Floru'). A strong-growing shrub. Single, deep violet-pink flowers have a deep red eye. (Bellion)

Hibiscus syriacus White Chiffon ('Notwoodtwo'). A strong-growing shrub with anemone-like, pure white flowers, each with a puff of stamenoid petals in the center. Winner of a Silver Medal from the Royal Boskoop Horticulture Society. (Woods)

Hibiscus syriacus 'William R. Smith'. Very large single flowers are pure white with crinkled petals.

Hibiscus syriacus 'Woodbridge'. Large single flowers are a rich rose-red with a bright red center.

Hardy Hibiscus Cultivars

Hibiscus 'Anne Arundel'. A compact plant with gorgeous clear pink 9-inch (22.5-cm) flowers and deeply cut foliage. (Darby)

Hibiscus 'Baboo'. Flowers are white and pink, with overlapping petals. Growth habit is compact. (Gilberg)

Hibiscus 'Becca Boo'. A bush with three-lobed foliage and handsome pink 10-inch (25-cm) flowers with a crimson eye. (Gilberg)

Hibiscus 'Blue River II' (Plate 34). Pure white flowers grow to the size of dinner plates. Very showy when in full bloom. (Winters)

Hibiscus 'Candy Stripe'. White flowers accented by red veins are 5 to 9 inches (12.5 to 22.5 cm) in diameter.

Hibiscus 'Clown'. Pink flowers are 5 to 9 inches (12.5 to 22.5 cm) in diameter, with fuchsia veins and a red eye.

Hibiscus 'Crimson Eye'. An early variety listed in a 1902 catalog. Flowers are white with a crimson center.

Hibiscus 'Crimson Wonder'. Flowers are a rich dark red.

Hibiscus 'Crown Jewels'. Compact plants produce slightly ruffled, pure white flowers accented with a crimson eye. Foliage is a lovely purple-green. (Fleming)

Hibiscus Disco Belle series. These dwarf forms of 'Southern Belle' grow to a height of only 20 to 30 inches (50 to 75 cm) with 9-inch (22.5-cm) flowers. Selections include 'Disco Belle Pink', 'Disco Belle Rosy Red', 'Disco Belle White', and 'Disco Belle Mix'. (Sakata)

Hibiscus 'Etna Pink'. Ruffled flowers up to 12 inches (30 cm) in diameter are light pink with a dark crimson eye. Leaves are reddish. Red stems provide winter interest. (Morrison)

Hibiscus 'Everest White' (Plate 35). White flowers up to 12 inches (30 cm) in diameter have a deep pink eye. This selection also features lush green foliage. (Morrison)

Hibiscus 'Fantasia'. A smaller plant that grows to only about 3 feet (0.9 m) tall, with a good rounded form. Leaves are palmate and maple-like. Large pinkish lavender flowers are 8 to 9 inches (20 to 22.5 cm) in diameter and very ruffled. (Fleming)

Hibiscus 'Fireball'. A compact rounded bush sometimes described as an improved 'Lord Baltimore'. Finely dissected leaves are green with a purplish red blush. Rich burgundy-red flowers are 12 inches (30 cm) across, with neatly overlapping petals. (Fleming)

Hibiscus 'Flare'. This improved sterile hybrid (one of the Texas Superstar series) is a prolific bloomer. Fuchsia flowers are large and showy.

Hibiscus 'Fresno'. Flowers are large and pink.

Hibiscus 'Giant Yellow'. An early variety listed in a 1902 catalog. Noted for its 9-inch (22.5-cm) canary-yellow flowers with a garnet eye.

Hibiscus 'Kilimanjaro Red'. Thick-petaled deep red flowers are up to 12 inches (30 cm) in diameter. Pointed leaves are basically oval in shape. (Morrison)

Hibiscus 'Kopper King'. White flowers with a crimson eye and red veins grow up to 12 inches (30 cm) in diameter, with some overlapping and ruffling. The three- or five-lobed palmate foliage is deep green overlaid with copper-red. The undersides of the leaves are quite orange-red. (Fleming)

Hibiscus 'Lady Baltimore'. Well-defined, 5-inch (12.5-cm), cone-shaped flowers are bright pink with a rosy eye. Foliage is deeply lobed. (Darby)

Hibiscus 'Lester Riegel'. Flowers are typically 5 to 8 inches (12.5 to 20 cm) in diameter. Pink flowers have a dark red eye and deep pink veins.

Hibiscus 'Lord Baltimore' (Plates 36 and 37). This striking plant grows up to 5 feet (1.5 m) tall and bears prolific bright red flowers. (Darby)

Hibiscus 'Matterhorn'. The 12-inch (30-cm) flowers of this 4-foot (1.2-m) plant are a rich rosy pink at the outer edges and white toward the center, which is marked by a red eye. Leaves are oval. (Morrison)

Hibiscus 'Mauna Kea' (Plate 38). A tidy busy with oval leaves and medium-pink flowers that reach 9 inches (22.5 cm) in diameter. (Morrison)

Hibiscus 'Mauvelous'. A compact plant that grows to just over 3 feet (0.9 m) tall, bearing 10-inch (25-cm) mauve flowers and dark foliage on maroon stems. (Gilberg)

Hibiscus 'Old Yella'. Pale creamy yellow flowers grow 10 to 12 inches (25 to 30 cm) in diameter, are slightly ruffled, and have a crimson eye. Leaves are ovate. (Fleming)

Hibiscus '100 Degrees'. A vigorous, compact plant with clear, light pink, 9-inch (22.5-cm) flowers. Petals overlap in such a way as to produce a swirling effect. Leaves are oval and serrated. (Gilberg)

Hibiscus 'Pitter Patti'. White flowers feature a small pink eye, red speckles, and pronounced veins. (Gilberg)

Hibiscus 'Plum Crazy'. Flowers are 7 to 8 inches (17.5 to 20 cm) in diameter and a rich plum to rose-purple with darker purple veins and an even darker eye. The staminal column is a contrasting yellow, and the maple-like leaves are purple-green. (Fleming)

Hibiscus 'Pyrenees Pink'. A vigorous grower and prolific bloomer with oval leaves. Flowers are 12 inches (30 cm) across and hot pink with a deep red eye. The edges of the petals are slightly darker than the middle. (Morrison)

Hibiscus 'Rainier Red'. Oval leaves are topped by huge 12-inch (30-cm) flowers that are deep crimson-red. (Morrison)

Hibiscus 'Rose Pink with a White Base'. An early variety listed in a 1902 catalog. As you might expect, flowers are rose-pink with a white base.

Hibiscus 'Southern Belle'. A popular crimson-flowered form that grows up to 4 feet (1.2 m) tall. (Sakata)

Hibiscus 'Southern Belle Mix'. Flowers are white, pink, pink and white, rose-red, and red. Winner of the All-America Selections award. (Sakata)

Hibiscus 'Sweet Caroline'. A perennial that grows 4 to 6 feet (1.2 to 1.8 m) tall and at least 3 feet (0.9 m) wide, with 6- to 8-inch (15- to 20-cm) flowers in several shades of pink. Brightly colored flowers have slightly darker veins, a darker eye, and petals that are slightly ruffled and partially reflexed. Flower buds resemble expanding rosebuds. (Winters)

Hibiscus 'Turn of the Century' (Plate 39). A handsome large plant that grows 6 to 8 feet (1.8 to 2.4 m) tall. Bicolored flower petals range from dark red to pale pink in lengthwise zones, giving the flowers a sort of pinwheel effect. Petals are slightly overlapping.

Tropical Hibiscus Cultivars

Hibiscus acetosella 'Red Shield'. Noted for its brilliant maroon foliage.

Hibiscus 'All Aglow' (Plate 40). A 3- to 6-foot (0.9- to 1.8-m) bush. Luminous yellow flowers are 5 to 6 inches (12.5 to 15 cm) across, trimmed a sort of caramel-brown, and white at the throat. Listed in the United States, Australia, and South Africa. (Kanzler)

Hibiscus 'Amanda Dubin' (Plate 41). A low-growing shrub. Yellow 8-inch (20-cm) flowers have a red eye and last for two days. This slow grower is well suited for containers and grows well indoors. Grow in full sun to partial shade. (Sinclair)

Hibiscus 'Amber Suzanne'. A medium-sized bush with long-lasting, double, white and pink flowers. Considered a noteworthy plant by experts. (Conrad-Shew)

Hibiscus 'Aurora'. Pom-pom flowers are soft blush-pink.

Hibiscus 'Blueberry Hill' (Plate 42). A fast grower that makes a great cover-up plant for outdoor growing in subtropical climates. Seven-inch (17.5-cm) flowers are pink with a light blue tint and represent progress in the breeder's search for a blue hibiscus. (Sinclair)

Hibiscus 'Bridal Veil'. Large single white flowers have a crepe-like texture.

Hibiscus 'Brilliant Red'. A reliable bloomer that may reach 4 to 5 feet (1.2 to 1.5 m) if left unpruned. Bright red single flowers are 5 inches (12.5 cm) wide. (Yoder)

Hibiscus 'Byron Metts' (Plate 43). A fast grower that will do best in partial shade. Pearl-white flowers last for two days. Considered a noteworthy plant by experts. (Sinclair)

Hibiscus 'Candy Wind'. Large pink flowers have ruffled edges and a dark pink stamen and throat. (Yoder)

Hibiscus 'Captiva Wind'. A naturally tall plant. Petals are an unusual pale lavender with dark pink outer edges. Glossy foliage is medium green and dentate. (Yoder)

Hibiscus 'Carolina Breeze' (also known as 'Caroline'). A compact plant bearing brilliant orange flowers that are 5 inches (12.5 cm) in diameter. (Yoder)

Hibiscus 'Chocolate High' (Plate 44; also known as 'Jim Berry'). A thick ever-blooming bush for warm climates. Flowers are a caramel-chocolate color, with a striking red and white eye, and are up to 5 inches (12.5 cm) in diameter. (Sinclair)

Hibiscus 'Cool Wind'. Flowers are white with a pink throat. Leaves are disease-resistant. (Yoder)

Hibiscus 'Cooperi'. Flowers are rose-red. Narrow, lanceolate, olive-green leaves are marbled with white, pink, and red.

Hibiscus 'Crown of Bohemia'. Fully double flowers are golden yellow with a flame-orange throat. (Vavra)

Hibiscus 'Dainty La France'. Large, single, nodding flowers are bright pink with darker pink veins and have lobed, frilled petals. Leaves are ovate and lobed. *Hibiscus* × *archeri* is thought to be a parent.

Hibiscus 'Donna Lynn'. Pink flowers have pale yellow edges and a red throat. (Howlett)

Hibiscus 'Dragon's Breath' (also known as 'Roy Kautz'). A reliable hibiscus for both indoor and outdoor culture. Single, ruffled, rose-red flowers have a darker throat. Considered a top plant by experts.

Hibiscus 'Fiesta' (Plate 45). Crinkled, single, 5-inch (12.5-m) flowers are flaming red at the center, with deep orange petals. Flowers last two days.

Hibiscus 'Fifth Dimension'. Bell-shaped flowers are whitish gray with white rays, yellow edging, and a dark red throat. This 6-foot (1.8-m) shrub was Hibiscus of the Year in 1989. (Howard)

Hibiscus 'Flaming Wind' (Plate 46). Flowers are soft red with a dark red throat. Foliage is an attractive dark green. (Yoder)

Hibiscus 'Golden Wind'. A continuous-flowering variety. Vivid yellow flowers contrast with a light orange throat. (Yoder)

Hibiscus 'Green Hornet'. An extremely ruffled red-throated hibiscus. Its yellow flowers have a hint of green, a rarity in hibiscuses. Named Hibiscus of the Year in 1994. (Goulding)

Hibiscus 'Herm Geller'. A medium-sized bush considered noteworthy experts. Single flowers are a soft honey-brown and gold with a red eye. (Ludick)

Hibiscus 'Kissed'. Vivid red flowers are large and single. Reflexed petals signal that this variety may have *H. schizopetalus* in its background.

Hibiscus 'Kona'. Flowers are double and pink.

Hibiscus 'Lady Elizabeth'. Magenta to pink flowers are up to 8 inches (20 cm) in diameter.

Hibiscus 'Lateritia Variegata'. Golden yellow flowers cap foliage that is heavily variegated white and green.

Hibiscus 'Mandarin Wind'. A compact plant with glossy foliage. Flame-orange flowers are 6 inches (15 cm) in diameter and feature a light pink band on the throat above a star-like red eye. (Yoder)

Hibiscus 'Miss Vermont' (Plate 47). A slow grower that does well in containers either outdoors in southern climates or indoors. Huge, double, red, orange-tipped blooms open above large, glossy, dark green leaves. Best planted in full sun to partial shade. (Sinclair)

Hibiscus 'Molly Cummings'. An easy-to-grow, half-hardy bush. Single red flowers are richly textured. (Parnell)

Hibiscus 'Peggy Henry'. Noted for its double yellow flowers, unusual for tropical hibiscuses.

Hibiscus 'Percy Lancaster'. Single flowers are pale pink with a hint of apricot and a russet eye. Petals are narrow.

Hibiscus 'Pink Versicolor'. A reliable plant that is compact if

pruned and medium-tall if unpruned. Bright pink 5-inch
(12.5-cm) flowers have a dark pink throat. (Yoder)

Hibiscus 'Pond Scum'. Some find this cultivar appealing, while
others consider it the ugliest thing they've seen. I had to include it for its name. Flowers are a greenish brown.

Hibiscus 'Ruby Brown'. Large, single, orange flowers are tinted
brown and have a dark red throat.

Hibiscus 'Ruth Wilcox'. Noted for its double white flowers, unusual for tropical hibiscuses.

Hibiscus 'Snow White'. Grows well in sun to partial shade. Snow-
white 8-inch (20-cm) flowers have a large red eye. (Sinclair)

Hibiscus 'Sundance'. Golden yellow 5-inch (12.5-cm) flowers fade
to white toward the center, then brighten with a star-shaped
pinkish red eye. (Yoder)

Hibiscus 'Sunny Delight'. Single flowers are bright yellow with a
white throat.

Hibiscus 'Superstar'. May reach 3 to 10 feet (0.9 to 3 m) if left
unpruned. Striking, bright yellow, 8-inch (20-cm) flowers
have a deep red throat. Considered a noteworthy plant by
experts. (Howard)

Hibiscus 'Texas Rose' (Plate 48). Lemon-yellow flowers are quite
double. The doubling is by ruffled petals rather loosely held
together. Leaves are dark green with smooth edges. (Sinclair)

Hibiscus 'Topsy'. Single golden yellow and red flowers top a
low-growing prolific bush. A good plant for beginners.
(Thompson)

Hibiscus 'Wedding Band' (Plate 49). Burnt orange to reddish
flowers are edged in yellow and reach 5 to 6 inches (12.5 to
15 cm) across. (Sinclair)

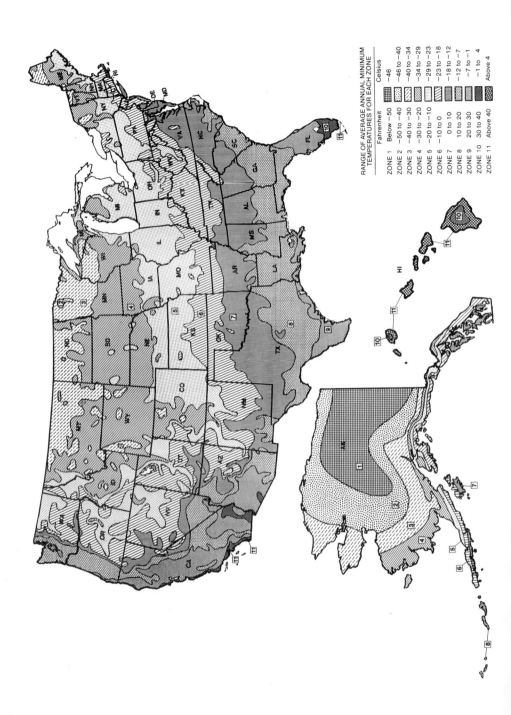

RANGE OF AVERAGE ANNUAL MINIMUM
TEMPERATURES FOR EACH ZONE

	Fahrenheit	Celsius
ZONE 1	Below −50	−46
ZONE 2	−50 to −40	−46 to −40
ZONE 3	−40 to −30	−40 to −34
ZONE 4	−30 to −20	−34 to −29
ZONE 5	−20 to −10	−29 to −23
ZONE 6	−10 to 0	−23 to −18
ZONE 7	0 to 10	−18 to −12
ZONE 8	10 to 20	−12 to −7
ZONE 9	20 to 30	−7 to −1
ZONE 10	30 to 40	−1 to 4
ZONE 11	Above 40	Above 4

U.S. Department of Agriculture Hardiness Zone Map

Major Societies and Nurseries

American Hibiscus Society
4231 Shamrock Drive
Venice, Florida 34293
phone: 941-408-9309
www.americanhibiscus.org

Australian Hibiscus Society
23/129 Albany Creek Road
Aspley, Brisbane, Queensland
Australia 4034
phone: (07) 3263 4232
www.australianhibiscus.com

Bluebird Nursery
P.O. Box 460
519 Bryan Street
Clarkson, Nebraska 68629
phone: 1-800-356-9164
fax: 402-892-3738
www.bluebirdnursery.com

Exotic Hibiscus
P.O. Box 158
Myakka City, Florida 34251
phone: 941-322-2841
fax: 941-322-2852
www.exotichibiscus.com

Hidden Valley Hibiscus
2411 East Valley Parkway, PMB 281
Escondido, California 92027
Phone: 760-749-6410
Fax: 760-749-8165
www.exotic-hibiscus.com

International Hibiscus Society
www.internationalhibiscussociety.org

Logee's Greenhouses
141 North Street
Danielson, Connecticut 06239
phone: 1-888-330-8038 or 860-774-8038
fax: 1-888-774-9932
www.logees.com

Plant Delights Nursery
9241 Sauls Road
Raleigh, North Carolina 27603
phone: 919-772-4794
fax: 919-662-0370
www.plantdelights.com

Stokes Tropicals
4806 E. Old Spanish Trail
Jeanerette, Louisiana 70544
phone: 1-800-624-9706 or 337-365-6998
fax: 337-365-6991
www.stokestropicals.com

Walters Gardens
P.O. Box 137
1992 96th Avenue
Zeeland, Michigan 49464
phone: 1-888-925-8377
fax: 1-800-752-1879
www.waltersgardens.com

Yoder Brothers
phone: 1-800-321-9573
www.yoder.com

Glossary

aculeate: bearing sharp spines; prickly.

ascending: rising upward, usually from a horizontal or slanting position.

axil: the upper angle of the joint between a stem or axis and a leaf, branch, or stalk.

basal: at the base or arising from the base.

bract: a modified leaf, often small and scale-like, that is usually part of an inflorescence and encloses the stem and flower bud.

calyx: a collective term for separate or joined sepals that form the outer whorl of the flower.

chlorosis: a diseased condition that causes foliage to turn yellow while the veins remain green, often due to an iron deficiency caused by soil pH that is too high.

cordate: heart-shaped.

corolla: the inner circle or second circle of the perianth or floral envelope, composed of either separate or fused petals.

crenate: scalloped, with shallow rounded teeth.

cultivar: cultivated variety, either selected from existing plants or purposely bred.

deciduous: shedding leaves once a year or at certain periods, usually in the fall.

dentate: toothed.

diploid: having the usual two sets of chromosomes, such as found in the original species.

dissected: deeply divided or cut.

downy: covered with short soft hairs.

elliptic: oblong and widest at the middle, with narrowed to rounded ends.

entire: having a continuous, unbroken margin.

epicalyx: false calyx or conspicuous bracts surrounding a calyx.

erect: perpendicular to level ground or another point of attachment.

evergreen: having foliage that remains green throughout more than one growing season.

filament: a thread-like part or organ, especially the stalk of the stamen that bears the anther.

genus (pl. **genera**): a taxonomic category that falls between family and species, comprising one or more species that share distinctive characteristics, and that is designated by a singular capitalized Latin word, as in *Hibiscus*.

glabrous: hairless, smooth.

habit: the general appearance and characteristics of a plant.

hair: an outgrowth of the plant epidermis that may be of several types according to its form, branching, and attachment.

herb: a plant with no woody stems aboveground; also, a plant with aromatic, medicinal, or savory qualities.

herbaceous: having stems and foliage that die back to the ground each year.

hybrid: a plant resulting from a spontaneous or purposeful crossbreeding of parents that are genetically unlike, usually belonging to different species.

internode: the part of a stem between nodes.

involucre: a circle of bracts, usually found beneath a flower.

lanceolate: lance-shaped.

morphology: the study of form and structure.

mutation: a sudden, often permanent, often obvious genetic change.

node: the place on a stem or trunk where leaves, shoots, branches, or flowers attach.

ovate: egg-shaped.

petiole: the stalk of a leaf.

pH: a measure of soil alkalinity and acidity, with 7 being neutral, higher numbers being alkaline, and lower numbers being acid.

pistil: a female reproductive organ of a plant, usually consisting of ovary, style, and stigma.

pubescent: covered with short, fine hairs.

raceme: an unbranched, indeterminate, usually elongated inflorescence with stemmed flowers.

serrate: saw-toothed.

simple: not compound or divided, unbranched.

solitary: occurring singly.

species: a taxonomic category that ranks immediately below the genus and that is designated by a binomial consisting of the genus name followed by the Latin, uncapitalized species name, as in *Hibiscus syriacus*.

specific epithet: species name, as *syriacus* in *Hibiscus syriacus*.

sport: an individual that is distinguished as a result of mutation.

stamen: the pollen-bearing male organ of a seed-bearing plant, consisting of anther and filament, though sometimes reduced to only the anther.

stigma: the apical part of the pistil that receives pollen and that usually has a different texture than the rest of the style.

stoma (pl. **stomata**): a pore or opening on the surface of a leaf that allows an exchange of gases.

style: the more or less elongated portion of the pistil between the ovary and the stigma; absent if the stigma is sessile.

subshrub: a shrubby perennial with stems that are woody only at the base; a very low shrub that is treated as perennial; a perennial herb with a woody base and somewhat soft stems.

subtend: to be below and close to, and often to enclose.

tetraploid: having four sets of chromosomes rather than the usual two sets.

triploid: having three sets of chromosomes rather than the usual two sets.

woolly: having long, soft, somewhat matted hairs.

Further Reading

Armitage, Allan M. 1997. *Herbaceous Perennial Plants.* Second edition. Champaign, Illinois: Stipes Publishing.

Armitage, Allan M. 2001. *Armitage's Manual of Annuals, Biennials, and Half-Hardy Perennials.* Portland, Oregon: Timber Press.

Bailey, Liberty Hyde. 1949. *Manual of Cultivated Plants.* Revised edition. New York: Macmillan.

Bailey, Liberty Hyde, and Ethel Zoe Bailey. 1976. *Hortus Third.* New York: Macmillan.

Balfour, Isaac Bayley. 1888. *Botany of Socotra.* London: Williams and Norgate.

Banks, Joseph, Daniel Charles Solander, and James Britten. 1900–1905. *Illustrations of Australian Plants Collected in 1770.* London: British Museum.

Brickell, Christopher, and Judith D. Zuk, eds. 1997. *The American Horticultural Society A–Z Encyclopedia of Garden Plants.* New York: D. K. Publishing.

Bown, Deni. 1995. *Encyclopedia of Herbs.* New York: Dorling Kindersley.

Buchoz, Pierre-Joseph. 1775–1778. *Histoire Universelle du Regne Végétal.* Paris: Brunet.

Cavanilles, Antonio José. 1785–1787. *Monadelphiae classis dissertationes decem.* Paris: F. A. Didot.

Chin, Hoong Fong. 1986. *The Hibiscus.* Kuala Lampur, Malaysia.

Curtis, William. 1790. *Curtis's Botanical Magazine.* Vol. 3. London: Royal Botanic Gardens, Kew.

Curtis, William. 1792. *Curtis's Botanical Magazine.* Vol. 5. London: Royal Botanic Gardens, Kew.

Curtis, William. 1793. *Curtis's Botanical Magazine.* Vol. 6. London: Royal Botanic Gardens, Kew.

Curtis, William. 1796. *Curtis's Botanical Magazine.* Vol. 10. London: Royal Botanic Gardens, Kew.

Dippel, Leopold. 1889–1893. *Handbuch der Laubholzkunde.* Berlin: P. Parey.

DiSabato-Aust, Tracy. 1998. *The Well-Tended Perennial Garden.* Portland, Oregon: Timber Press.

Dobelis, Inge N., ed. 1986. *Magic and Medicine of Plants.* Pleasantville, New York: Reader's Digest.

Fryxell, Paul. 1988. *Systematic Botany Monographs.* Vol. 25, Malvaceae of Mexico. American Society of Plant Taxonomists.

The Garden, Vol. 6. 1874. Royal Horticultural Society.

Garden and Forest, Vol. 1. 1888. Garden and Forest Publishing.

Gardeners' Chronicle, Vol. 4. 1844. London.

Gast, Ross H. 1967a. The Genetic History of *Hibiscus rosa-sinensis. Journal of the Royal Horticultural Society* 92 (8).

Gast, Ross H. 1967b. Hibiscus: Queen of the Flowers. *Journal of the Royal Horticultural Society* 92 (8).

Gast, Ross H. 1980. *Hibiscus around the World.* Pompano Beach, Florida: American Hibiscus Society.

Geological and Natural History Survey of Minnesota. 1897. *Minnesota Botanical Studies.* Minneapolis: Harrison and Smith.

Gerard, John. 1597. *The Herball.* London: John Norton.

Gledhill, D. 1989. *The Names of Plants.* Second edition. Cambridge: Cambridge University Press.

Gray, Asa, and Isaac Sprague. 1849. *Genera Florae Americae Boreali-orientalis illustrata.* New York: G. P. Putnam.

Griffiths, Mark. 1994. *Index of Garden Plants.* Portland, Oregon: Timber Press.

Humphrey, Donald. 2001. All-American Mallows. *The American*

Gardener 80 (4): 29–34. Alexandria, Virginia: American Horticultural Society.

Irwin, Howard S., ed. 1996. *America's Garden Book.* New York: Macmillan.

Jacquin, Nikolaus Joseph. 1770–1776. *Hortus Botanicus Vindobonensis.* Vienna: J. Kaliwoda.

Jacquin, Nikolaus Joseph. 1781–1793. *Icones Plantarum Rariorum.* Vienna: C. F. Wappler.

Knowles, G. B., Frederic Westcott, and William Smith. 1837–1840. *The Floral Cabinet and Magazine of Exotic Botany.* London: William Smith.

Kopp, Glenn, ed. 2002. *Integrated Pest Management.* St. Louis: Missouri Botanical Garden.

L'Héritier de Brutelle, Charles Louis, and Pierre Joseph Redouté. 1784–1785. *Stirpes, Novae, aut Minus Cognitae.* Paris.

Newcomb, Lawrence. 1977. *Newcomb's Wildflower Guide.* Boston: Little, Brown and Company.

Palmer, Stanley J. 1997. *Palmer's Hibiscus in Colour.* Runaway Bay, Australia: Lancewood Publishing.

Rumpf, Georg Eberhard. 1741–1750. *Herbarium Amboinense.* Amsterdam.

Salisbury, R. A., William Hooker, and D. N. Shury. 1805–1807. *The Paradisus Londinensis.* London: William Hooker.

Sauer, J. D. 1993. *Historical Geography of Crop Plants.* Boca Raton, Florida: CRC Press.

Schloss, Sue, ed. 1990. *The Hibiscus Handbook.* Lake Worth, Florida: American Hibiscus Society.

Scopoli, Giovanni Antonio. 1786–1788. *Deliciae Florae et Faunae Insubricae.* Pavia, Italy.

Walker, Jacqueline. 2001. *Hibiscus.* Willowdale, Ontario: Firefly Books.

Winters, Harold F. 1970. Our Hardy *Hibiscus* Species as Ornamentals. *Economic Botany* 24 (2): 155–164.

Index of Plant Names